THE WAY OF THE MONK

THE WAY OF THE MONK

bringing the spiritual into everyday life

by Vincent Cole

Desert Monk Press
Tucson, Arizona
monksbook.com

ISBN-13: 978-0692231258

ISBN-10: 0692231250

Library of Congress Control Number: 2014942616

Printed in the United States of America

"Who can leap

the world's constraints

and sit with me

among the white clouds?"

—Han Shan

Contents

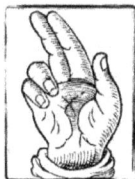

PEACE TO ALL WHO ENTER

Many people are searching for greater meaning in their lives. Many are seeking a greater understanding of themselves, the world around them and the spiritual realm beyond.

To those who truly seek, enter the pages of this book with an open mind. The Way of the Monk offers understanding, as well as practical advice by illuminating the ancient techniques of the monk adjusted for present-day life.

No matter what the circumstances of your life, you can still follow the Way of the Monk. Even if you have family commitments and financial responsibilities, even if you are obliged to live and work in the world, you can adopt monastic practices in your everyday life.

The simple Way of the Monk will guide you along an inner journey that will develop and enhance the soul's innate spiritual abilities. With some time, effort and practice, the Way of the Monk will expand your awareness not only of the world around you, but most importantly, also impart greater appreciation of your journey on earth.

But first —

What is a Monk?

Images arise: sandals, tonsure, a rope for a belt; fat, jolly friars partial to frothy beer; gaunt, hooded ascetics with a fondness for self-flagellation; Saint Francis as a perch for birds, a lone figure silently standing in a garden; saffron robes mottled by a green forest; red robes chanting the sutras in ornate temples. Some images are true. Some are fiction. Always male. I guess women who follow The Way are referred to as nuns.

But as Saint Jerome once said, *"Interpret the name monk, it is thine own. . ."*

To be a monk is to follow an uncharted path. It is a journey of discovery, a quest to find the source of the river. Along the way, he or she may stop to test the water, to gauge its clarity and determine what direction to take.

A monk, however, does not stop to build a church along its banks or form an organization to advance the expedition. The quest leaves little time or energy for worldly matters.

A monk will forsake a personal family but sees all people encountered on the journey as a brother or sister. Nevertheless, a monk often walks alone. A monk has few friends. Few companions are willing to also search for the source of the river.

A monk is celibate so to be blind to the world of duality, seeing neither male nor female, neither old nor young, neither beautiful nor ugly, seeing not the flesh, but the light of the soul.

A monk lives simply treating possessions as cumbersome burdens. Though grateful for all that is given, he or she remains detached.

A monk is imperfect. Only God is perfect and a monk seeks perfection through God.

A monk is a child who will stumble. Monks know they will trip over his or her mistakes. Chastity, simplicity and devotion are all practices and like someone learning a musical instrument, the wrong note will often disturb the harmony but the monk continues to practice.

The Way of the Monk is difficult. Obstacles get in the way. Sacrifice is painful. Confusion lurks at every new turn in the road. Nevertheless, the monk will continue to walk and stumble because the monk is homesick. Home for a monk is not a place but a state of being.

Some will see the monk as mad or foolish. Some see only the images found in picture books and movies. Look closely and see the scarred bare feet from thorns trampled underfoot. Feel the ache of loneliness when no one listens, the tear-filled eyes that have seen suffering in the world, the broken body that has struggled to free itself from the trap of trivialities.

Look closer, however, and you will also see a smile. For the monk who has found the source of the river is given *"what no eye has seen, no ear has heard, what no hand has touched, and what has not arisen in the human heart."*

The Way of the Monk

is like a tree with vast roots always growing
with branches that touch every region in the universe
with diverse fruit both sweet and bitter.
Some will attempt to climb its highest branches
while others are content to rest in its shade.
But all are able to taste its golden fruit
and be nourished by its nectar.
Each bite brings a new flavor
while the last taste lingers.
The juice nourishes the soul
comforts the body,
calms the mind
and strengthens the heart.

The Call

"The call does not come to the ear,

but to the heart.

One does not hear it as much as one knows it."

—Fulton Sheen

No one knows when a soul begins to yearn for something more, to soar above the mundane and feel once again the sacred light of its birth. The soul is eternal and is not constrained by hours, days and years. Exactly when the soul makes itself known, by what methods it asserts itself, is a mystery. Just as some plants await the warmth of summer to flower and others blossom in autumn while still others need the quiet of winter, every soul has its season.

When the time comes, the soul makes itself known in different ways. Some people feel restless. Everything around them seems small and stifling. Family, friends and career become burdens of responsibility. They become irritated with routine and try to find a way to add excitement in their lives. When that doesn't work they become angry, quick to blame others and are tempted to make radical changes.

The restless ones will someday understand it is their soul that feels trapped. It yearns to fly rather than crawl. It seeks a view from a greater height. If they listen carefully, they will hear the voice of the soul asking, "Is there more to life than this?"

For other people, the soul stirs deep within the abyss of emptiness. In their hearts and minds, life has been stripped of all meaning. Something is missing. Something is lost. Neither pain nor joy is felt. There is only a pervading apathy. Life for them is just a matter of going through the motions of existence.

There is a sense of alienation, as if an invisible barrier exists between them and the rest of the world. They are always on the outside looking in; thinking everyone else holds the secret to a joyful life. Those who experience the cold depths of emptiness often lose hope. Many blame themselves, wondering what is lacking in their lives, what deficiency exists that makes them different. Even their reflection in a mirror becomes meaningless. The face looking back is that of a stranger.

In an attempt to feel alive, they will seek out physical sensations of both pain and pleasure. They grasp at any quick answers only to be disappointed when the solution fades into the abyss and a new "cure" must then be found. The promises of the world soon prove to be nothing more than fancy gift wrap with gold ribbons covering an empty box.

The soul, however, does not settle for trifles. Once all that is superficial and meaningless is stripped away, the soul can emerge. Within the void, its small persistent voice asks, "Who am I?"

For many others, the whisper of the soul is heard in the midst of tragedy. In one horrific moment, life is altered. What was once cherished is gone, ripped away so painfully that no defense, no reasoning of the mind and no amount of comfort can lessen the grief.

Great misfortune leaves a wound that seems impossible to heal. It aches with feelings of helplessness, anger and fear. Life seems chaotic and dangerous. Anything can happen. People no longer feel in control of their lives, yet they will try to recreate life as it was before tragedy intruded. They will try to put together the broken pieces into some semblance of normalcy. Nevertheless, something will always be missing. Something is forever gone.

Attempts to regain the past by clinging to memories or to continue as if nothing happened can only numb the sorrow of a broken heart. The soul, however, awakened by pain and tears, relentlessly cries out, "Where is God?"

From the depths of the emotions, the soul calls out and speaks of another way of being in the world.

Whenever it happens, however it comes about, the soul makes it way through the labyrinth of the mind and struggles with the diverse and complex physical sensations of everyday life.

The struggle of the soul can be like a trickle of water slowly gaining momentum until it becomes a stream and then a river surging toward the ocean. Or, it can be like a volcano gathering force for many years then rumbling forth in a grand explosion. It can be nagging, uncomfortable, irritating or compelling as it breaks through the barriers of mind.

Like Lazarus called forth from the tomb, the soul answers the call to life as it rises from the darkness of limited beliefs into the light of a greater awareness.

It struggles because there will be resistance. As it emerges out of the depths, it must confront the stone sealing the entrance to the tomb. The stone blocking the way is fear.

The soul seeks another reality that often contradicts the beliefs of the physical self. The conscious mind, developed and reinforced for many years, creates for itself a system of beliefs and defense mechanisms formed by its experiences in the temporal world. By focusing on material reality, perception is limited to what can be seen, heard or touched. But life is more than the body. The soul is eternal and gives testimony that there is more to life. A greater reality exists when all that can be seen has fallen away, when all that can be heard is silenced and when all that the hand touches turns to dust.

When the soul begins to express itself, the spiritual often conflicts with the physical. The soul challenges the beliefs and defenses of a mind focused solely on the world. To heed the call of the soul can be difficult, at times more painful than can be imagined. But the greater sorrow lies in ignoring the needs of the soul. To suppress spiritual potential is to deny an additional source of energy, wisdom and love.

Denying its existence, resisting the soul's struggle to be heard causes conflict and pain when the two forces collide. The greater the resistance, the greater the split within the heart, mind and body.

Once the stone dividing the two realms is removed, however, what seemed like contradictory forces become complimentary. In the material world, the soul is edified by its experiences on earth. In turn, the soul guides physical actions in the world towards a greater good.

Allowing the soul to have its say is a rebirth. The emergence of the soul as an active participant in the world brings about personal transformation. It transmutes the primitive into something sacred. As carbon is transformed into a diamond, the soul seeks the same metamorphosis as it purges impurities that may darken its God-given light.

The soul knows it is eternal. As such, it is always in communication with the source of all life. Therefore, it knows there is more to life than what the physical senses perceive and will struggle through the turmoil of everyday life, calling out to be heard above the noise of physical existence.

To answer the call of the soul is to look deeper within the heart not of muscle and blood but the eternal heart of the soul in love with God. The soul seeks to feel that love. Just as a child delights in the embrace of its mother, the soul rejoices in the love of God.

Listening

Consider these words: *"I have called you out of the world,"* said the Rabbi Jesus, who is called the Christ.

Obviously, if you are reading this book something is stirring within you. Even if only mere curiosity, still that is enough. Therefore, take some time away from the world. Take some time for yourself.

You may know what the world wants from you, what family and friends expect of you, but to know yourself, to truly feel what is within you, takes quiet introspection.

Do not wait to find the time. Insist upon it. Go for a walk or a drive. Hang a "Do Not Disturb" sign on your door. Don't answer the doorbell. Ignore the telephone. It is not selfish to give yourself time. It is wisdom.

As Christ said, *"Man does not live by bread alone."*

You are, after all, more than a physical body. You have a soul. Is it not worth the time and effort to develop what existed before you came into this world and will remain when the body is finally abandoned to the earth?

- 15 -

What is forgotten is the incontestable truth that the struggle for physical survival is a losing battle. In the end, only the soul remains. It will depart this earth strengthened by its experiences, enhanced by wisdom gained and purified by sacrificing one state of being for something greater.

Or, neglected and starved, the soul will be weakened by spiritual poverty.

The soul becomes ineffectual when the needs of the body are given greater attention because the demands of the physical self are easily recognizable and quickly satisfied if only for that moment. When it is hungry, it is given food. When cold, it seeks out warmth. When pain is felt, the body yearns for comfort.

So it is with the soul. Neglected, it becomes hungry. Ignored, it becomes cold. In its weakened state, it cries out to be comforted.

Yet, much more time and effort is spent taking care of the physical body though its true purpose is misunderstood. The body is the physical instrument through which the soul expresses itself on earth. Every soul has an agenda. Earthly existence is its classroom. By experiencing physical reality, the soul learns, develops and grows. A birth certificate is nothing more than a temporary student visa.

Just as flesh and blood has its needs, the soul also hungers for nourishment. Nurturing the soul is a continual process that is not always easy. There will be times of grace and times of challenges. You must accept both. Those who lack courage will flee from the first obstacle.

It doesn't matter, if you presently feel that the required strength is beyond you at this time. Help will be given. Spiritual muscles will develop. just as you can strengthen the body's muscles through exercise, the Way of the Monk will fortify the soul.

All you need to begin is willingness. Take a moment to consider your desire. Even a small amount will do, for like a small mustard seed, it will grow in time. Be honest with yourself. Be neither overconfident nor self-effacing in your examination but examine your true thoughts and feelings.

If disbelief exists, so be it. You can stop there or search deeper. If there is fear, feel it but don't trust it. Fear can block you from discovering your deeper feelings. Fear separates you from experiencing a connection to the sacred.

If, on the other hand, you feel confident in what you've already learned in life and are comfortable with your present situation, then you deny yourself new experiences.

Most of all you must ignore any feelings of unworthiness. Accept that your soul is a spark of God's light manifesting in this world. It is precious. Know that God's love is like the sun that shines on all, regardless of past mistakes.

Your efforts are not an attempt to earn God's love. You have that already. The Way of the Monk rolls away the stone so the light of God's love can be felt. This light illuminates not only your own being but also the world around you.

To heed the call of the soul is to transform your life, to experience profound changes in your development as a human being walking upon the earth. Such changes will transform your thoughts, your actions and your perceptions of life.

Take time and make the effort for the sake of your soul. It can only add to you in immeasurable ways.

Remember that the physical body can only decrease for that is the nature of earthly reality. Only the arrogance of self-delusion does humanity expect to outlast the trees and mountains. But the soul is eternal and the riches of the heart will endure when all else is finished.

Right now, in this fleeting moment, take what time you need to consider the challenges and rewards of answering the call of the soul. Feel it stirring within you. Your soul beckons you towards a new direction in life, a narrow path leading to new experiences and a greater awareness.

Take time to consider the crossroads upon which you now stand.

Saint Antony of the Desert

is considered the father of the monastic family.

He was born about 251 A.D. in Kemn-el-Arouse in Egypt. At the age of 18 his parents died. Antony sold the family's lands and possessions and gave the money to the poor.

At first, he studied with a holy man on the outskirts of town. When the holy man died, Antony went into the desert and lived in an ancient tomb carved into the side of a mountain. Many years later, he moved to another mountain near the east bank of the Nile, living in complete solitude within an abandoned fort, confronting temptations and demons. Word of his holiness spread and many sought him as their spiritual leader.

Dawn's faint light etched deep shadows on a barren mountain. Nocturnal creatures scurried to their dens as birds ruffled their feathers, restlessly awaiting the full light of sunrise. A young man, exhausted by countless days wandering the desert until he found the mountain, slowly took the final steps to the place he long sought and the man many spoke of but few people saw.

Now that he finally arrived, the young man was unsure. He was tired. His feet were bleeding. Worse, he was stricken with doubt and fear.

He stood in the shadow of a crumbling old fort, its walls outlined in the faint light of daybreak. The place looked haunted by ghosts and devils. He had heard stories. It was said the old man within often battled with hell's creatures.

A huge boar with fiery eyes and sword-sharp tusks, a lion with a snake for a tail and stinking of rancid meat and a winged demon with long talons took turns tormenting the holy man, grasping him by the beard and lifting him into the air. When he was hungry, they presented a feast of costly foods. When cold, the demons presented blankets of soft fur. When he felt lonely, they offered him the warm embrace of a woman's soft arms and legs.

Each time the holy man refused, resuming his prayers and hours of meditation as the demons howled in frustration.

It was also said the holy man spent the past twenty years in self-imposed solitude. He never left the fort and never invited anyone in. Nevertheless, men and women gathered on the mountain, living in caves and flimsy huts. They sought his advice and guidance even if spoken through a barred wooden door.

The young man was the latest to cross the desert and climb the mountain. At that moment in the pre-dawn light, with the ground still cold and damp beneath his sore bleeding feet, the young man could no longer remember why he had traveled so far. He wanted to turn around and return home but he was hungry and tired so he knelt at the door and wept.

Through wet, red eyes, the young man saw the pale golden light of the sun slowly climb the walls of the fort. He slept a little or imagined he did. He dreamt a little or it just seemed like a dream when the door opened and an old face peered at him.

A subtle breeze stirred long white hair and beard the way the wind causes clouds to drift. The face looking through the door was lined and dirty like sandy driftwood but the eyes were young and gentle, the smile as sweet as a mother's compassion. Yet there was also a serious wildness to the face, a primal strength radiating in the air with pulsating waves like the shimmering heat of the desert. "What troubles you, young soul?" The voice. A wind blowing through a canyon. A dove calling. The sharp rolling crash of a rock falling down the mountainside.

The young man wiped tears and dust from his face. "I've come to see the holy man Antony but I am afraid."

"Of what?"

"I don't know." The words suddenly rushed out of him, a torrent carried along with his tears. "I've traveled far but I didn't mind. My feet compelled me to keep going. I couldn't stay where I was, couldn't live not knowing. I want to know God. I want to know the truth. I prayed and prayed. Then I walked and walked. Always searching but never finding. Now I think my quest is impossible."

The old man stepped through the open door and helped the young man to stand.

"Fear not," Antony said. "The goodness you seek is not an impossible thing. Nor is it set at a great distance from you. It hangs upon your own determination."

Antony reluctantly left the fort. He knew it was time.

It is written, "The Lord gave Antony grace in speech so that he comforted many in sorrow. Others who were at strife, he made friends and through him the Lord healed many who were suffering and freed others from evil spirits."

The Way

"If you would be a monk, you must be content,

for Christ's sake, to be esteemed a fool in this world."

— Thomas a Kempis

The Way of the Monk transcends cultural and religious affiliations. It is as universal as it is timeless. The Way is open to all: women and men, regardless of their station in life. It is a way of life that has no barriers, no distinctions as to gender or race, social standing or education. All are equal. All share in the benefits. All come to know the same love.

The term 'monk' was never an ecclesiastic title. It was a word given by people to certain individuals living apart from mainstream village life. The word itself is believed to come from the Anglo-Saxon mumuc, derived from the Latin word monachus, which in turn stems from an ancient Greek word that could be translated to mean alone or single.

Monks were the solitary ones. They separated themselves from tribal activities to go in search for answers to ancient mysteries. They were the men and women who left the company of others to live in a cave or a graveyard, to wander the vastness of the desert or settle in huts within the depths of the forest.

The solitary appearance of a monk is not one of isolation but of joining countless others who have directed their attention away from complicated worldly concerns. Monks only seem cut off from common life because they are less involved with the physical world in order to develop and enhance their spiritual abilities.

The hermit in the desert, the small groups of men and women chanting psalms, the apartment dweller quietly saying a rosary, every monk is listening to the call of the soul. Though the Way of the Monk is varied and rich, every monk follows an ancient path where the unseen is revealed, the unspoken is valued and mysteries fade in the light of understanding.

The Way of the Monk is an inner journey. It is nothing less than the quest for holiness. Prayer, contemplation and acts of devotion are the traditional exercises of a monk. These practices are as essential as eating and sleeping. Used on a daily basis, they nourish and strengthen the soul.

As the exercises of prayer, contemplation and devotion are food for the soul, the sacred vows of humility, simplicity and chastity are disciplines for the mind and body. These sacred vows guide a monk's interaction with the world. These exercises and vows help the monk discover a greater dimension of earthly existence. The Way of the Monk awakens the soul and its dormant abilities. Monks experience an increased sensitivity and a heightened awareness of holiness infusing all of creativity.

In heeding the call of the soul, a monk places restrictions on his or her physical activities in the world. Instead, a monk builds a personal monastery as a sanctuary dedicated to spiritual pursuits. Time spent alone with God in prayer, contemplation or acts of devotion can be more enriching within a sanctuary away from distractions and interruptions.

A monastery, however, is more than stone walls and a locked gate. It is something monks build within themselves. The locked gate symbolizes the wisdom of discernment, choosing what you are willing or unwilling to do in the world. The flowers in the monastic garden are your thoughts. The chapel is your heart.

The Way of the Monk brings faith to replace worry and fear. It gives strength to vanquish weakness and self-destruction. The Way offers peace to calm anxiety. The supremacy of love deposes hate and heals the conflicted heart. The treasures of the soul compensates for any material deficiency.

Be forewarned, however, there will be difficulties. A monk not only has to face personal resistance but also possible rejection from others. It is not unusual for family and friends to feel threatened as you make changes in your life. A new address or a new career are easily acceptable but to turn inward, to begin a spiritual request is often misunderstood. After all, the rewards of the world are perceivable to the human eye. An increased paycheck, a new home, the latest fashion in clothing are things that can be seen, touched and appreciated.

To follow the Way of the Monk will take strength and perseverance. Not only will people in your life misunderstand you, there will be times even you will be confused by your actions and unfamiliar feelings. Like any explorer entering unknown terrain, the monk explores and discovers deeper levels of the self and a greater awareness of reality.

The Way of the Monk is not for those seeking ease and comfort. There will be times of difficulty. Strength will be needed as the world continues making its demands. In the world, there are many distractions. Something is always calling out for attention: the ringing telephone, the unpaid bills, the social and family commitments, job requirements and more. Countless decisions have to be made. Daily chores need to be done.

Therefore, the inner strength of the soul must be awakened. The power of the soul is stronger than physical muscle or intellectual aptitude. The vows and practices of the monk calls forth this inner strength and sustains it.

The Way of the Monk takes time and practice. The beginning may be confusing and frustrating, even painful. Know, however, you will not be alone in your efforts. Know that all of heaven rejoices when a soul struggles beyond worldly limitations

to reach the light. As you struggle out of the darkness of ignorance, helping hands surround you, beckoning, assisting and protecting you on the journey. Have faith in the invisible forces helping you and have faith in yourself.

Advisory

Be Forewarned: The Way of the Monk is not for everyone.

Traditionally, anyone seeking to enter a monastery must first go through a trial period. Not everyone was accepted.

There was no judgment in sending someone away. It was done as much for the sake of the individual as it was for the stability of the monastery.

A mentally unstable person would find the Way of the Monk too confusing, which would aggravate a troubled mind.

A postulant in severe emotional turmoil would feel conflict and discord rather than peace.

Someone seeking to hide from the world will not find a refuge, only disappointment.

The Way of the Monk is not a cure-all. Nor is it a formula for a carefree life. The Way has its own unique challenges. The message of this book offers only guidelines along a path leading to sacred exploration and soul-discovery.

Use them wisely. Practice the exercises with sincerity.

If at this point, however, it's only curiosity that has you turning the pages, so be it. A decision to adopt the Way of the Monk is not required. Let the words be like seeds that will take root in its own time.

If, on the other hand, you have heard the call of the soul wanting more out of life, then take from these pages what will inspire the mind, excite the heart and direct your energy towards a new direction in life.

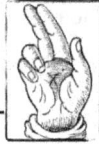

Syncletica of Alexandria

In many ways, the life of Syncletica of Alexandria is similar to that of Antony Abbot. Like him, Syncletica was born into a wealthy family. Also like Antony, when her parents died she gave her possessions to the poor and left the city. For years she lived as a hermit residing in an old crypt beneath an abandoned church. Local people spoke of her holiness and many women who visited Syncletica heard the call of their souls.

In time, a community of women formed under her guidance. They called her "Amma," their Spiritual Mother (men were called Abba, meaning father). It is believed she died at the age of 80 around the year 350 AD.

Three women from different parts of Egypt went into the desert to see Amma Syncletica. Though they left at varying times and traveled by different routes, they all arrived at the hermit's crypt at the same hour on the same day.

Amma Syncletica greeted them, standing in the harsh sunlight, shading herself with a palm frond. Her skin was burnt as brown as a ripe date. Her long hair was streaked grey by time and dust. She wore a cloak of woven palm leaves, dry and brittle, that would soon need replacing.

When the women asked to join her community, Amma Syncletica said she would have to speak to them privately before she could agree.

The first was a woman from Alexandria who carried a basket crammed with scrolls. "I have studied with many teachers and read the works of Philo, Apollos and Marcion," the woman said. "I've learned so much but still have many questions. For example, according to this treatise by Papias of Hierapolis, he writes——"

Amma held up her hand. "Before we begin," she said, "grant me a small favor. Go within my hermitage, the crypt behind you, and start a fire in the brazier."

"A what? Did you say build a fire? In this heat?"

"Yes. There is wood and flint within."

"But I've never built a fire. I've always had servants to do such things. Besides, I've come a long way seeking guidance and wisdom. If we could just discuss——"

Amma turned and walked away.

The second woman was young and enthusiastic. She started talking as soon as Amma drew near. "I've been a devoted daughter of the Lord since I was a little girl. I fast every holy day. I am charitable to the needy. I pray on my knees first thing every morning and at night by my bedside. I so much want to be holy like you."

Once again, Amma held up her hand. Again, she made the request: build a fire in the crypt.

The young woman hurried into the darkness of the crypt as Amma sat upon a rock and waited. She didn't have to wait long. Smoke streamed from the cavity of the crypt. The young woman soon followed, coughing and wiping her red eyes.

"I'm sorry, Amma," she said with words punctuated with wheezing and hawking. "The wood must be too green or wet. I'd just got a spark going and the whole place filled with smoke. Oh my Lord, I'm almost blind from it. I couldn't stay in there a moment longer."

Amma walked away without saying a word. The young woman was confused and called out to her. "But Amma, if you could just tell me which prayer or act of devotion merits the most good I'd be grateful."

Amma did not turn around nor did she speak.

She found the third woman patiently waiting.

"Is there anything you want to discuss?" Amma asked her.

"No."

"Then, is there some specific instruction you seek?"

"No, Amma."

"What then do you want?"

"Nothing. I mean, it's enough just to be near you."

Amma stared at the woman for a short while before instructing the woman to do as the others. The woman merely nodded and went down into the crypt.

After a short while she emerged, her face smudged with soot, her eyes streaming tears but she was smiling. Without saying a word, Amma Syncletica took the woman by the arm and led her to meet the sisters of the community.

Later, she was asked why she put people through a test of fire. Amma Syncletica replied, "All must endure struggle and conflict when first approaching God. But afterwards, there is inexpressible joy. It is just like building a fire. In the beginning, it is smoky and your eyes water, but afterwards you achieved the desired result. It is written, 'Our God is a consuming fire' and so we must kindle that divine fire within ourselves with effort and tears."

Humility

"Even if you are otherwise perfect,

without humility you fail."

— The Talmud

True humility is like walking a tightrope strung across two illusions. On one side is the individual wanting to be special, someone who could do no wrong. On the other side is the self-depreciating individual carrying a burden of faults and flaws. True humility is a path between the two, staying balanced with sincere honesty.

To stay honest, there must be an openness to truth. True humility is simply being honest as to who you are and who you are not. In social settings, masks are worn as a form of identity. Clothing, hairstyles, makeup, manners of speech are all part of a self-created identity. Much of this creation is a result of a person's experiences in the world.

Many people think their experiences made them who they are. In reality, it is actually their reactions to those experiences that have formed their beliefs about life and so became the building blocks to a personal identity. Experiences, however, are nothing more than events that happen in a person's life. Many people have similar experiences and yet, reactions differ.

Some people will construct an overly confident personality. They are certain of their beliefs, never questioning their actions and defensive towards anything that challenges their carefully crafted self-image. They are only open to information and experiences that will reinforce and support their beliefs.

Other people, most often those deeply wounded by the harsher experiences on earth, will lack feelings of self worth. They see their 'failures' in life as their own fault. Fearful of life, some will try to create a safe environment as protection. Others will attract experiences that will reflect and reinforce their beliefs of worthlessness.

Of course, there are varying degrees of both manifestations of self-identity. Both forms, however, are reactions to the concept of 'a perfect life.' If only (fill in the blank) would happen then life would be perfect. If only I had more money, if only I met my soul mate. If only I could lose weight or had a better education or lived somewhere else.

Seek perfection and you will be disappointed. A humble monk is not called to be perfect but is called to develop the soul. A monk seeks the perfection of God in spite of his or her personal imperfections.

Consider the words of a monk who was asked what he and his fellow monks did all day. He replied, "We wake up in the morning and walk. We fall down. We get up again and walk again knowing we will fall, knowing we will get up."

This is known as 'stumbling towards God.'

Only in God is there absolute perfection. Therefore, a humble monk leaves perfection to God and seeks perfection through God. The Way of the Monk is not the quest for personal excellence but the desire to see and be a part of the perfection of creation.

Aware of his or her own human imperfections, accepting them as part of the great experiment of life on earth, a monk is less likely to judge the faults of others. Instead, a humble monk's efforts are spent removing the beam from his or her own eye rather than focusing on the speck of dust in the eye of someone else. Being humble and using strength removes the beam and the monk's eyesight will be clear. Only then can the monk be of service to others.

Strength and humility are not opposites but complimentary. Without humility, strength easily becomes arrogance. Yet, humility without inner strength can be self- defeating. False humbleness suppresses a monk's abilities.

A monk strives to be aware of both his or her weaknesses and abilities; humbly removing limitations and flaws while strengthening the soul's capacity to radiate light where there is darkness, to bring laughter where there is sorrow, to bring understanding where there is confusion. In all he or she does in the world, the monk remains humble.

In this great circus called life, the monk walks a tightrope strung from this world to the next. Patiently, one foot is placed in front of the other. Sometimes she stumbles. Sometimes he falls. Doing so teaches the monk that he or she has leaned too far in the wrong direction.

Again, the ladder is climbed. Again the swaying dance continues. Balance is found through practice and the monk will learn to walk upon clouds as easily as on the ground.

Consider the words of Christ. *"Whosoever exalts himself shall be abased and he that humbles himself will be exalted."*

Personal glorification is a fragile pedestal built on temporal values. Wealth, physical beauty, talent and intellect have an end. The praises of family, friends and society are soon silenced. All the trappings cherished by the ego are left behind at the grave. As an Italian proverb states, "After the game the king and pawn go into the same box." Whether in a pauper's unmarked grave or a stately marble mausoleum, the result is the same.

Those who seek to exalt themselves are primarily concerned only with the self. Their thoughts and actions are selfish, even when disguised with a veneer of altruism, promising to be charitable if given wealth, claiming to serve God as justification for their ambitions. Because so much of their energy is spent on self-glorification, their awareness and experiences will be limited.

Because the values of the world are fragile and temporary, standing on a pedestal is isolating and precarious.

Those who humble themselves, however, do so with an awareness and understanding of eternal wealth that can never be destroyed.

Beyond the Self

Spend just one evening looking at the stars. Know that the earth is not the center of the solar system. The planet you stand upon, along with billions of others, is not the center of the universe. Consider the vastness and intricacy of creation.

Understand you are a small part of its beauty. Become aware that you are connected to everything you see—the ground beneath your feet and the most distant of stars. You are also a part of all you cannot see—the angelic powers flowing through the universe and the history of all that has been and the birth of what will be.

Be humbled by this knowledge and let the entire universe embrace you as a portion of creation.

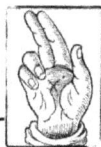

The First Steps of a Young Seeker

A young man heard the call of his soul and asked the wise men of his village the way to God. They gave him books to read but it was not enough. He then went to the temple priests who taught him rituals but the young man was not satisfied.

One day as he wandered in the marketplace he heard a traveling merchant speak of a holy man living deep in the forest. The young man left the next day.

After a month-long journey and getting lost several times, the young man came to a thatched hut almost undetectable among ancient oak trees. A man with long unruly hair and a beard like moss on a tree sat in the doorway weaving a basket out of reeds.

"Greeting Grandfather," the young man said. "That's a beautiful basket you're making."

The holy man looked up. "It's taken you a long time to get here, my son. What is it you want?"

"I want to live a holy life. Please Grandfather, show me the path to God."

The holy man nodded then continued his weaving. The young man waited. When the basket was finished, the old man stood and pointed towards the west.

"Not far from here there is a village. West of the village is a graveyard. Go among the graves and praise those who are buried there."

The young man was perplexed but did as he was told. He had read how teachers will test a person before accepting them as a student.

He easily found the graveyard and was grateful the place was deserted.

"How fortunate you all are to be free of this world of turmoil and hardship. The goodness of your lives has brought each of you to heaven and now you enjoy the company of angels. Because of the good deeds you did on earth, you now dwell among the saints. I honor you for being true sons and daughters of the Most High."

He continued walking among the tombstones and praising the dead. After several hours, he returned to the hut in the forest.

"I've done as you requested," he told the holy man, who just nodded and said, "Now return to the graveyard and curse them."

The young man walked slowly back to the graves wondering if the old man was holy after all. Maybe the long journey had been in vain. With each step, his doubts increased.

He asks me to first praise and now curse the dead. What is the point. Perhaps the old man crazy. This is all a mistake. Maybe I'm a fool to stand in a graveyard talking to the dead. Maybe I should just go home. Then again, maybe this is a test of my obedience.

Once again, among the graves, the young man cursed the dead. "You wasted your lives on earth. All of you are great sinners, foul and evil. You rot in your graves, nothing but food for worms. At least now, you're good for something. The world is a better place without any of you."

When he finished cursing them, their ancestors and their offspring, the young man returned to the holy man who was weaving another basket. Without looking up, he asked the young man, "Did you do as I asked?"

"Yes, Grandfather."

"Did you praise the dead?"

"I did."

"And then did you curse them?"

Yes, I praised them and then I cursed them."

"How did they react?"

The young man was now convinced the holy man was indeed crazy.

"They didn't react at all. Not to my admiration or my condemnation."

The holy man looked up and smiled. "Very good. Now, if you want to be holy then you must be like the dead. Ignore the honors and insults of men and remain true to your own path."

Simplicity

"How many undervalue simplicity.

But it is the real key to the heart."

— William Wordsworth

Simplicity is the art of seeing an entire garden within a single rose. It is the ability to see the earth in a mere pebble and feel the expanse of the universe when looking at a distant star.

Simplicity is not so much the scarcity of material possessions, but the enrichment of the self through an enhanced awareness that sees beyond mere appearances.

By sacrificing complicated involvements and possessions that no longer have a purpose, you gain time and energy to turn your attention towards spiritual matters. Making sacrifices, however, will not be easy.

Possessions have become extensions of an individual's identity. People create a false sense of self-worth by adorning themselves with the chains of material goods. Every item is a reflection of the image they want the world to see. Simple cooking utensils become an outward display of status. Clothing becomes a statement. Brand names have more importance than one's own given name. Technology that didn't exist a month ago swiftly becomes a "must have."

The need for something more, something new is perpetuated, packaged and sold. Consumer appetite is stimulated by a bombardment of advertising. Social acceptance is sharing values and the agreement that certain possessions are an outward sign of belonging.

This is most often seen with younger people when they begin to separate from their families and form other social bonds. Dress, language, hairstyles and shared beliefs mirror others in order to be part of a peer group. This mind-set continues to a larger or lesser degree in adulthood.

When taken to an extreme, people become what Buddhist iconology depicts as "Hungry Ghosts," creatures with small mouths, long thin necks but enormous stomachs that can never be filled, never be satisfied no matter how much the ghost manages to eat.

Therefore, remember the words of Jesus.

"Do not lay up for yourselves treasures upon the earth where moth and rust corrupt them and where thieves break through and steal. But lay up for yourselves treasures in heaven where neither moth nor rust corrupt and where thieves do not steal. For where your treasures be, there will your heart also be."

Remember, you came into this world with nothing and will leave with nothing. Where then is your self worth? What happens to your identity? You are more than flesh and blood and you are worth more than the objects you acquire. See all material items for what they are. Clothing, pots and pans, artwork, the house you live in are just things, some useful, others not. Most of all, none of those things are you. But they do have an effect on your physical, mental and emotional condition.

Useless possessions weigh upon you, holding you to the earth. Every object has a vibration, whether you're conscious of it or not. The more objects surrounding you, the heavier the atmosphere. Everything you own keeps you focused on the material world. Even items hidden away from sight are not forgotten but remain in your memory, knowing they can be retrieved if and when the need arise.

Of course, some people find comfort in an abundance of material goods. There is, however, an inherent wisdom within the conscious mind that knows everything could suddenly vanish. Things become outdated, can break, become rusty, be stolen or lost. Natural forces like fire and flood can take everything away in a single moment. Though much pleasure is gained from "pride of ownership," there is also a degree of insecurity, as well as a compulsion to protect the self by safeguarding purchased treasures, which are priceless in life but worthless in death.

Other people get a thrill acquiring new possessions. There's a feeling of accomplishment. For a while, the new item fills an empty space in the person's life. In time, the feeling fades and something new must be sought and purchased. In the extreme, such people become hoarders, filling their living space and their lives with mountains of cherished "necessities."

Even in small amounts, possessions become burdens when there is an emotional attachment. Most often, it's the connection to a past event in the person's life: a childhood cherished toy, a gift from a beloved, an item that brought joy during a difficult time.

Such possessions fetter a person to the past. Consider how burdensome it would be to walk forward if you're looking behind you, focused more on where you've been than where you're going.

Because of this strong emotional association, many people find it a struggle to relinquish items that no longer serve a purpose in their lives, except as a memory of what once existed. How much more difficult and painful it will be when forced to let it all go?

Time will take it all away. Death will steal it from you.

The material world has much to offer. Possessions do have a purpose. Clothing protects the body. Food needs to be cooked. Technology aids in communication. Children need toys. An artist needs brushes and paints. A monk has a use for items that help meet his or her physical and spiritual requirements.

Even the beauty of a single rose has its purpose.

It's when the acquisition and maintenance of possessions become too important, become confused with self-worth and self-identity, then each item becomes a link in a heavy chain. You are then shackled to a limited perception of reality, seeing only the fleeting material world.

Realize that any possession, like a single rose, will someday lose its beauty and fragrance. Your true worth, however, will remain forever.

Breaking Chains

To cope with an increasingly complex world, humanity developed selective eyesight and constrained awareness. This is most evident in large cities. The human mind would be overwhelmed if made to see and acknowledge every passerby, every passing car, every window in a skyscraper. An individual has to discern quickly what is relevant and ignore all the rest.

This ability to walk through life with blinders on is a relatively recent development in the human experiment. In order to survive, the human species had a more expansive awareness, sensitive to the slightest movement, attuned to the softest sound. Life depended on a far-reaching awareness for hunting and gathering food while avoiding predators at the same time.

But the human experience was simpler then. Nevertheless, the capacity for an extended awareness remains within each individual. The Way of the Monk is to awaken that ability. An expanded awareness sees more in the world, both its physical and spiritual manifestations.

Begin by removing anything in your life that is no longer necessary. Take some time and examine your personal surroundings, things openly on display and those items hidden away from sight. Ask yourself as you gaze at each thing, whether or not there is a true need for it. The "need" doesn't have to be practical. If an object brings beauty and joy into your home, then keep it.

If something has been broken for more than six months, then obviously you have no need for it. Throw it away. If you have clothing you no longer wear, consider giving to a charity. With everything in your life, ask yourself if perhaps someone else has a greater need for it—then donate whatever no longer has a meaning or purpose in your life.

For most people, the difficult part in letting go is eliminating any items with an emotional attachment to the past. To do so will truly be a sacrifice.

Emotions are a part of you, a valuable aspect of being human. But with items that evoke an emotional response to an event in the past, what you feel are just shadow emotions, remnants of a poignant experience. Clinging to that item can never recreate the event and the initial emotional reaction.

When you feel the struggle to let go of a cherished item from days gone by, simply remind yourself that it's impossible and self-defeating to live in the past when so much more awaits you.

Simplifying your life by discarding what is useless not only frees you from the dictates of consumerism, you also create a space where new experiences are welcomed.

If these words make you feel reluctant, ask yourself why.

If you feel hesitation, then wait for a time when there is willingness.

If you feel the process of simplifying your life as something impossible, remind yourself that someday you will have no choice but to let it all go. Why wait?

Remind yourself that there is more to life. Know that your self-worth does not depend on material abundance that fades away all too quickly.

Break the chains that keep you bound to this world.

You are more than the things you own.

The most valuable thing you have is your soul.

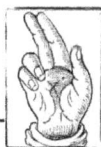

A Lesson in Value

Several students went to see a Sufi teacher. When they arrived at the teacher's home, they found all the chairs, couches and cushions already occupied by the local villagers so they sat on the floor and waited.

They expected the teacher to speak on the Koran, to share his interpretation of some key passages. Instead, the teacher opened his hand to show everyone a palm full of gold coins.

"Who wants this gold?" he asked.

Everyone raised their hands.

The teacher then spit on the coins and asked, "Now who wants this gold?"

All hands stayed in the air, even the students who were confused by the actions of this so-called wise teacher of Islam.

The teacher then threw the coins on the floor. He took dirt from a flowerpot and threw it on the gold. Then he stomped on the coins.

"Anyone still want this gold?"

All hands stayed up. Everyone still wanted the coins.

The teacher laughed and threw the coins into the air. As people scrambled to catch the gold, the teacher said, "Remember this moment always, especially during times of trouble. Even though I had spit on the coins, covered them in dirt and stomped on them, they are still valuable. So it is with all of you. In all our lives, there are times when we are crushed, kicked, maltreated and insulted. In spite of that, we never lose our true worth."

Chastity

"The essence of Chastity

is not the suppression of lust

but the total orientation

of one's life towards a goal."

— Dietrich Bonhoeffer

Whereas, the practice of Simplicity is the sacrifice of useless objects, the practice of Chastity is an inner purging of thoughts and actions that are obstacles to spiritual growth. The goal of Chastity is to restore purity and innocence, to be like a child with faith, humbleness and the openness to learn from new experiences.

That does not mean giving up wisdom gained from the experiences of life on earth. After all, Christ did say, *"Be as innocent as a dove and as wise as a serpent."* This seemingly contradictory approach is easily explained.

Wisdom is not only knowledge gained from worldly experiences but also the innate awareness of the soul. It is the ability to see with clarity. The Way of the Monk is not just a journey towards a greater realization and expanded awareness. It is also a journey away from beliefs that inhibit your thoughts and actions.

When the pain of previous experiences is healed and when judgments of those experiences are erased with new understanding and heart-felt compassion, then you become as innocent as a dove.

Understand it is impossible to walk upon this earth without getting a bit dirty. In Buddhist symbolism, purification is washing away the dust of the world and returning to your original nature.

Consider what thoughts, beliefs and actions are not of your own creation but patterns developed since childhood, either imposed upon you or willingly adopted. Even belief-systems you rejected are based on your reactions to other people's beliefs and, therefore, are a limited and subjective viewpoint. Some of your cherished beliefs may have been useful in the past. Most, however, are of a limited perception about reality based on narrow experiences.

Chastity is the elimination of beliefs that no longer serve you. It is forsaking the habitual routines of daily life. It is sacrificing some experiences in order to redirect your energy towards a different goal.

One example of sacrificing experiences for something greater is the vow of celibacy. The redirection of sexual expression is just one component of Chastity, the most difficult and misunderstood portion.

Some people choose celibacy as a spiritual discipline; renouncing of their sexuality in accordance with religious dictates. Others have celibacy imposed upon them by disease, old age, death of a spouse or experiences of sexual abuse when fear damages desire.

Many people think celibacy means repressing sexual urges. For most people who live a celibate life, it is negating sexuality energy. To stifle that energy may work for some individuals, however, it can also be dangerous.

Sexuality is natural. It is a part of the human experience and for a reason. It is necessary for continuing the species and for physical pleasure. But it's an energy that can also be transmuted towards a spiritual purpose.

Sexual energy is the base vibration of what is called, the first or "root" chakra (The Sanskrit name for it is Muladhara) and is centered at the base of the spine. In the West, we call emanations of this energy feeling "horny," or "frisky" or other colorful and often accurate words to express the sexual

urge. The energy of the first chakra is important. It is your connection to the earth and the fire within which strengthens the physical body. Suppressing that energy is like pouring water on a fire that warms and energizes you.

Instead, it is better to feed the fire with a different fuel. Transformation of sexual energy is easier than imagined once it is no longer bound by limitations. The flexibility of this energy is most apparent in its lesser expressions as seen with sexual fetishes that channel sexuality towards specific objects and actions unconnected to actual copulation.

As sexuality can become distorted, it can also be taken to a spiritual level. The same energy that can be mentally fixated on experiences that seem unrelated to sexuality can also be transformed for other purposes, such as healing the self or others.

Sexual energy is a force. It is a fire giving power on different levels. It keeps you rooted to the earth and at the same time can transform your personal vibration to a new frequency.

Celibacy is not for everyone. When an individual is called to forgo sexuality, he or she does so in order to devote their lives towards another goal. Those who can re-direct that energy do so in the quest for personal transformation.

With eyes free from the blinders of physical desire, you will no longer see female or male, young or old, beautiful or ugly. You see only the soul.

And you will be filled with amazement at the beauty you see. As Christ said according to the Gospel of Saint Thomas, *"I marvel at how this great wealth has come to dwell in this poverty."*

Chastity is the discovery of that "wealth" which exists within the physical form. It is the ability to see that which exists once all else turns to dust. Most of all, it is feeling not just the love between two people, but also a love for all creation. Chastity is washing away the dust of this world, which is heavy and blinding. It is allowing the purity of the soul to emerge.

Transformation of the self, the elevation of internal and external energy, must take place on all levels. It remains incomplete unless the mind, body and emotions are in harmony with the spiritual. This takes great effort, determination, as well as patience and a willingness to suffer.

It is a struggle. It is a sacrifice. It is nothing less than a renunciation of self-centered pleasure, relinquishing the personal desires of the ego to discover something greater.

Transformation can be painful. You will stumble many times. As the old self is diminished, you'll feel self pity, anger and defiance. In order to emerge from the limitations of human conditioning, a death must take place. A part of you must die.

Whatever aspect of Chastity you endeavor to embrace, know that it will be difficult. Letting go of long-endured and cherished thoughts and actions that no longer serve you, whether it by embracing celibacy or by cleansing your self-identity of useless beliefs, will take time, patience and determination.

In the beginning, as you try to transform energy, beliefs and habits tend to get stronger because your thoughts are focused on that area. Whatever you try to relinquish, will seem strong and deeply rooted. Habits will tug at you, nag you and wear you down until you give in. This is often called, "falling into temptation."

But it is only the beginning steps of the transformational process. Be patient.

Think of life as playing a musical instrument. The practice of Chastity is like learning a challenging musical score. You will make mistakes, play the wrong notes and not get the rhythm correctly. And so, you start again. You practice. Eventually, your mind and body will learn to move in a different way.

Transformation can be achieved. You only need to be willing to step into the sacrificial fire and rise from the ashes. Once you do, beautiful wings will be yours. With those wings, you will reach new heights. Your vision will be greater and your awareness expanded beyond the self, beyond the world, beyond time and space.

Consider the words of Richard de San Victor: *"If you wish to search out the deep things of God, search out the depths of your own spirit."*

The Way of the Monk is taking time for periodical self-examination. Traditionally, monks would spend time in quiet introspection and public confession. Not an easy thing to do. It takes humble honesty and great courage to look within the depths of your own being.

Most people keep so busy they don't have time to examine their thoughts and actions. Using the time and energy gained by simplifying your life, take a moment and look at yourself with objectivity and not judgment. Be forewarned, to do so will be challenging.

You may not like what you see. Not if you are honest. Understand that humanity is not perfect and you are not flawless. In the great experiment of life on earth, there is much trial and error. All religions provide guidelines through Commandments, Sutras, Scriptures, and so-called "deadly sins." This was done to aid humanity in its growth from a primitive to a more advanced consciousness.

Those guidelines, however, were accompanied by a complicated system of prescribed punishments: purgatory, hell, bad karma, a lowly reincarnation, etc. Fearing "God's anger," many people are either encouraged or deterred from facing the human frailty that exists within all people.

Being motivated by fear has its limitations and is unnecessary. Fear of Divine Wrath invokes shame, guilt and oppression or it creates a defensive stronghold blocking out truth and avoiding repentance of detrimental behavior.

Repentance means changing your ways. Change of action results from a shift in perception. Going deeper than superficial judgments made about yourself and the world around you is finding the untarnished gold beneath the dust.

Have faith, not only in a Higher Power but also have faith in yourself. Know you have the ability to make the changes necessary. Do not doubt you have the strength to face challenges. Keep searching within and you will find the light of your own soul.

Purification

Consider the words of Christ: *"Every branch in me that bears not fruit He takes away and every branch that does bear fruit, He prunes so that it may bring forth more fruit."*

When something just begins to emerge, a potential habit or routine that is destructive, it is easy to eliminate it by simply snapping off the young branch and casting it aside. With deeper, more identity-rooted beliefs and actions, however, the process takes longer and is often more difficult.

The older the vine, the harder the wood. You decide one day that it must be cut down and you begin to hack away. Yet the vine is thick and the bark is tough. You can only cut so far. Perhaps on the first day you cut deep enough and the leaves whither and fall.

You assume the vine is dead and can now be forgotten. You walk away satisfied. Nevertheless, the vine once again grows and you are acting and reacting in the old ways. Don't be disappointed. The hard work you did was not in vain. Don't think the vine is too strong to be removed and therefore, will be a part of your life forever.

Some people will even try to rationalize the existence of the fruitless vine. They will defend it, saying it has a right to grow unhindered. They will go even further by encouraging it. After all, it is easier to nurture a useless vine than to uproot it. They will ignore how its roots deplete their power, how the branches and leaves cast great shadows that engulf and stifle growth of anything else.

For those who choose to tend the garden of their lives, they must return to the task. Again, they must start cutting away all that is barren. They must cut deeper. There will be times when spiritual forces come to help in the task, if called upon through prayer. And there will be times of rest. But each time an old way manifests itself, it is a time to prune away the old branches.

Remember, the vine took time to root itself and grow. It will take time and effort to uproot it. Each time you cut away at the branch, you gain strength, determination and discipline. The tools you use are the spiritual gifts of compassion, wisdom and understanding.

The compassionate way is knowing that what you are experiencing, any so-called flaw or sin or whatever you call it, is a part of the human experience on earth. You are not alone in this. Many others have experienced the same.

Wisdom is knowing how and when to cut, how deep you should go and when to rest from your labors. Wisdom gives you the discipline needed to purify the body, mind and emotions, removing what is harmful to your spiritual growth. It is knowing that the fruitless vine impacts all aspects of your life by reaching deep within you and influencing your decisions and actions.

Time will be needed. Uprooting the vine in a sudden upheaval can be devastating. Purification encompasses the mind, the emotions, and the physical body. Your body has become accustomed to the vine, has adjusted to its presence though it may be suffering because of it. Therefore, the body, along with the mind and emotions, needs time to adjust. Be aware that the body requires time to heal. In some cases, the affects of the dying vine are felt with flu-like symptoms, headaches or general weakness. Emotionally, there is often a feeling of emptiness and a vulnerability that comes from experiencing a loss. If not given time to heal, a person may feel disoriented and depressed.

Be patient and accept that there will be temptations to return to the old ways. Be aware, it will be difficult and even painful, especially at first, however, each time you cut away at the vine it will get easier.

Should you feel discouraged at times, evoke these words of Saint Thomas Aquinas and make them your prayer.

"Bestow on me, O Lord, my God, the understanding to know you, the diligence to seek you, the wisdom to find you and the faithfulness that may finally embrace you."

Remember always: The Kingdom of God is within you. Cut away the overgrown vines and you will find it.

Two novice monks went into town to purchase a few necessities for the monastery.

While they were in town the two monks had the occasion to sin (exactly what they did was not recorded).

On their return to the monastery, they argued about whether or not to confess the transgression to the Abbot.

"It wasn't so bad," the older one said.

"But it wasn't right," said the younger.

"We haven't taken our vows yet."

"Well, I'm still going to tell the Abbot."

"Can't you just forget about it? It wasn't so terrible."

"I have to confess. It's alright if you don't want to come along. I won't mention you."

"No, I'll go with you. But I wish you'd change your mind."

The Abbot heard their confession and told them to live as hermits for one month, fasting and praying. The two did as they were told, taking up residence in distant caves.

At the end of the month, the Abbot went himself to bring them back to the monastery. When they emerged from the caves, the Abbot was surprised by how different they looked.

The older novice who was reluctant to confess came out looking grim and downcast. His skin was pale and there were dark circles under his eyes. The other novice, however, appeared radiant and was smiling.

"What did you meditate upon?" the Abbot asked them.

The sad novice answered, "I could not stop thinking of the punishment that awaited me for having sinned."

The smiling novice said, "I thought of God's mercy and the love Jesus Christ had for all sinners."

The Abbot bid them both to return to the monastery to continue their studies. He embraced them and said, "I prefer a sinful monk who knows his faults and is humbled than a self-complacent monk of virtue."

The Song of Prayer

"In prayer, it is better to have a heart without words

than words without a heart."

— John Bunyan

Traditionally, monks schedule their voices according to a prescribed schedule of liturgy, prayer and casual conversation. Some religious orders adopt the discipline of silence, using sign language in place of words. When they do raise their voices in prayer, each word of every chant is all the more powerful.

Prayer is the voice of the soul singing to the world, to the universe, to God. It is an echoing song heard throughout time and space, an ancient melody of the hopes and desires of all humanity.

Every prayer has its own harmony: the lulling repetition of a chant, the crescendo of worship, the strident call for help and the soft hymn of gratitude. The soul hears the music of creation and adds its voice through prayer. Trees trembling in the wind, the roaring waterfall and the crackle of a fire, all are the earth's prayers of praise. All of creation resounds with the prayer of gratitude to its creator.

When the soul sings its song of prayer, it acknowledges and reaches out to something greater than itself. Wonder, awe and joy bring forth the soul's song. Like a child's surprised and delighted laughter at something beyond comprehension, the soul lifts its voice as it gazes on incomprehensible splendor and is stunned by its magnificence.

In the presence of overwhelming beauty, the soul sings out in appreciation and admiration. A prayer of devotion comes from the heart. The words spring forth. It is a song of love.

Prayers of veneration come not from the depth of anguished supplication but from the highest love.

Prayer is difficult to those who have never seen the splendor of creation. Such beauty seems hidden to eyes focused downward. Staring at the littered pavement, the stars go unnoticed. The veil of despair, the blindness of cynicism, the clamor of the world bombarding the mind stifles the song of the soul.

Instead, the mind wonders, 'What is there to sing about? Where is the beauty amid the intrusive sights and sounds, the swirling mass of images filling billboards, flashing neon signs and flickering television screens?'

But the soul knows the radiance of its own light and its connection to Divine and so will sing out in prayer. Its voice is the music of the litany, the lullaby of the chant, the chorus of a rosary and the soothing refrain of a mantra. Occasionally, it is the sound of a single word of pulsating power echoing throughout the universe.

Variations on a Theme

The First Octave

The most often used prayer is the spontaneous cry for help. It is the prayer of petition imploring divine intervention to save a life, to cast away misfortune or regain something lost. The soul strains against the confines of earthly existence, bursting through its silent cocoon, begging Divinity to come to its aid.

When the stronghold of the conscious mind is overwhelmed by tragedy, confusion and circumstances beyond its intellectual abilities, the soul speaks through the shattered heart and seeks God's help. Prayers of petition are not the last resort of the weak and infirmed. Such prayers are borne out of wisdom.

The soul humbly acknowledges its own limited abilities and therefore, seeks support from greater forces, from the saints and angels and from God.

And yet, these prayers are not always answered. As to why remains a mystery. One glimpse into that mystery is the understanding that not all prayers come from the soul, not all prayers comply with a greater wisdom. When it is the mind acting on its own, expressing its own desires through prayer, it is like a child begging for candy. It craves the momentary sweet taste of success rather than seeking nourishing food.

Some people profess a religious concept that abundance is a blessing from God. They pray for fame, money and physical prowess. The implication, of course, is that the rest of the population, those who fall short of reaching lofty goals are somehow unworthy or, for some reason, have been ignored by God.

Let the words of the Rabbi Jesus be remembered. *"What is thought highly of by men is offensive in the sight of God."*

True sincere prayer is the soul's longing to be nourished not by things that fade in time, but by the eternal light that flows throughout creation. Sincere prayer comes forth out of the "inner chamber," the place where the world does not intrude. From the depth of the heart, that secret place often ignored by the world, the soul speaks to God and hears the music of the universe. It then adds its voice to the timeless hymn.

The Second Octave

The second form is the ritual prayer heard in the repetition of a rosary or in droning chants and rhythmic mantras. Most religions implement this form. Hindus, Buddhists, Catholics and others use strands of beads; every bead is a prayer and every prayer is a single note played repeatedly. The last word in the prayer leads back to the first.

This form of prayer, however, is not just saying a set number of prayers within a certain time. In this form, the soul synchronizes with the rhythm of creation, the cyclical song of the changing seasons, the rotating and orbiting journey of the planet, the circle of birth, death and renewal. The loop of beads used to assist in this form of prayer amplifies the circular harmony of universe.

By repeating words in a cycle, the logical mind is quieted, lulled into a single focal point, concentrating on a solitary thought and one purpose. No longer focused on personal desires or divided by the countless concerns of the world, the mind is brought into sync with the song of the soul.

The mind in harmony with the rhythm of creation withdraws from the time and space restrictions of the world. Its focus turns inward as scattered thoughts are harnessed and subdued. Once tamed, the conscious mind relinquishes dominance and allows a deeper awareness to surface. Often this type of prayer becomes a doorway to the meditative state.

In unison with the soul, the mind discovers a greater awareness of reality. Soul and mind working together adds greater power to the prayer. The divine energy flowing through the soul gives the words of the mind the power to transform, to heal the body and make holy the mundane. More is brought about by prayer than can be imagined.

The Third Octave

Once the mind is calm and all personal intentions, desires and earthly concerns are abandoned, the third form of prayer spontaneously expresses itself. Personal identity is relinquished and you become an instrument through which the eternal song of prayer can be sung.

Every part of your being becomes the song.

It is a prayer without words.

You are the prayer.

This form of prayer is a song without beginning or end. Though only a single note in the celestial chorus, its sound is pure and strong. Those who experience this all-encompassing prayer know they are resonating to a higher tone.

Your entire being hears the sound of creation and raises its voice in accompaniment. You are not the originator of the song only a participant. Just as oceans sing upon the shore, as the wind plays its melody in the trees, as the sun and moon chant and the universe dances to the eternal hymn, the wordless prayer bursts forth with a simple and pure refrain. In the resounding choir of creation, the soul is heard to sing, *"God, let your will be done."*

How to Pray

The third form of prayer is reached in stages. It cannot be taught. Patience and persistence are disciplines needed just as musical scales are practiced before tackling a complicated concerto. Feeling the yearning of the soul to sing and calming the mind through a routine of prayer, are the beginning notes needed to reach the crescendo.

The music of prayer comes from the heart. When the heart is free, the song comes easily. A sincere prayer of the soul is uncomplicated. It is as simple as a conversation with a good friend. Begin by speaking to your friend with simple but meaningful words.

Consider the prayer given to us by the Rabbi Jesus. The simplicity of words, the purity of thought and the intimate approach gives power to the words.

Our Father who is in Heaven,

Holy is your name.

Your kingdom come

Your will be done

on earth as it is in Heaven.

Give us this day our daily bread

and forgive us our trespasses

as we forgive those who trespass against us

and leave us not in temptation

but deliver us from evil.

The spoken word has power. It can bless or curse, soothe or inflict, glorify or defile. As the Rabbi pointed out, it is not the things that enter the mouth which cause harm. It is the words which stumble forth *"from the heart. . .it is these things which make a man unclean."*

Words, therefore, should be used with wisdom. The angry heart speaks with bitterness. The cold heart voices words of hate. The broken heart speaks with fear. The protected heart is mute.

Prayer can be the balm that heals the heart.

And so, the first stage in developing a life of prayer is self-consecration. Begin by finding a prayer that has meaning, a prayer that touches you in a significant way. The prayer is for you alone, a keepsake held in a secret place, safe from the opinions and judgments of others. Think of it as a pearl of great value not to be displayed indiscriminately.

Find a prayer that appeals to the heart and not the mind. In this initial stage, you are setting a foundation and a complicated prayer, top heavy with ornate phrases, fanciful imagery and intellectual complexity is an unnecessary burden. Therefore, in choosing a prayer, keep it simple and easy to remember. The number of words does not matter so much as the focus you give them.

Remember, prayer is not to be an inconvenience or a chore. It is a reward you give to yourself. Prayer is time spent in a quiet, loving conversation with the Divine.

Once you have chosen a prayer, read it silently and contemplate its meaning. Also consider the time and place you will spend in prayer. In a monastery, the schedule for prayer has changed little over the centuries. In the world, you may have to be more flexible.

Find a time of day that you can truly make your own. For some people morning is ideal. Before starting the day, prayer prepares you, raises your vibration and keeps you mindful of what is important as you step out into the world. Others might find nighttime best for praying. When the world is at rest and stars in the sky testify to the magnificence of creation, a prayer brings peace. Some people, however, will have to grasp at any moment possible and a quick prayer is better than none at all.

Whatever time you find for prayer, keep it sacred and protected. Avoid distractions. Ignore interruptions. Insist on having time for yourself. Be careful about being undermined by others. Either consciously or by chance, people may try to intrude on your time. They will have to understand, perhaps even be inspired by your resolve to add the practice of prayer in your life.

Start by making a commitment to reciting your personal prayer for at least 15 consecutive days. The 15-day commitment is an act of self-dedication. During that time, the prayer merges with the psyche, becomes incorporated with your mind, body and soul. If a day should go by and you've forgotten, then add an additional day.

The practice of prayer is exactly that—a practice. Just as a musician takes the time to learn the notes, rhythm and pitch of a particular musical piece, so does the practitioner of prayer takes the time to learn the fundamentals until it becomes a natural, free-flowing utterance that echoes throughout the day.

Before you begin, take a moment and just relax. Put all other thoughts aside and say the prayer aloud. Being alone and speaking aloud may seem awkward but speaking and hearing the words benefits you. It helps you feel the meaning of the words. So speak the words loudly or softly, whatever best suits the moment. Then remain still and quiet. Assimilate the moment as the prayer establishes a connection from the timeless element within you to the eternal aspect of the universe.

You may not feel it at first. Maybe not after 15 days. Remember prayer is not an incantation or magical formula bringing instantaneous results by its mere recitation. On the other hand, by taking time and having patience to practice, prayer becomes powerful. Dedication and sincere effort transforms prayer from spoken words into a vital force that illuminates the soul.

When your entire being is taken up in prayer, you add your voice to the music of angels, the enduring song of the universe and the immortal harmony of all that is sacred.

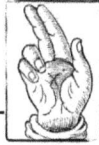

A retelling of a story by Leo Tolstoy

The Russian writer Leo Tolstoy (1828-1910) sought to change his lifestyle according to his code of spirituality. He gave up drinking and smoking, became a vegetarian and dressed as a peasant. His upper-class family did not agree to these changes. His wife was against his insistence upon chastity. She managed to obtain sole ownership of all his property including the copyrights to all his pre-1880 writings in order to provide for their large family.

Later in life, Tolstoy yearned for the monastic life where he owned nothing and could devote himself to service. He left home one night in search of a monastery that would take him in. Several days later, Tolstoy was found dead at a remote railroad junction. He was 82 years old.

A Bishop was sailing with a number of pilgrims on their way to visit shrines. The voyage was smooth and the weather favorable. One day, the Bishop saw the pilgrims talking to a fisherman who was pointing to a distant island.

The Bishop asked about what the fisherman had to say.

"He was telling us about the hermits," replied one of the pilgrims. "On that island are three hermits who live for the salvation of their souls."

"They are holy men," another pilgrim said. "I have heard stories about them. The fisherman was telling us how one stormy night he got stranded on the island. In the morning, he discovered a small hut of dirt and driftwood. The three hermits fed him and dried his things, then helped him mend the boat."

"What are they like?" the Bishop asked.

"One is a small man with a crooked back. He wears a priest's cassock. Some say he is more than 100 years old. The second is also very old but he is taller and wears the tattered coat of a peasant. The third has a white beard that reaches to his knees. He wears nothing but a tunic made of woven reeds."

"I would like to meet these men," the Bishop said and he went off to speak to the captain of the ship.

The captain tried to dissuade him. "The ship this size cannot get close to the island."

"Can I not be rowed there in a small boat?"

"Yes, I suppose that would be possible," said the captain, "but you shouldn't go through all that trouble. They are only old foolish men who understand nothing and never speak much to anyone."

"Nevertheless, I would like to see them. Please arrange it and I will pay for your trouble."

Within the hour, a small boat with the Bishop accompanied by a young sailor to do the rowing was lowered over the side. As they approached the island, the Bishop could see the three old men standing on the shore. Apparently, they had seen the boat and were waiting to greet their visitors. The old men bowed as the Bishop stepped out of the boat and gave them his benediction.

"I have heard about you three," the Bishop said. "It is said you are godly men living on this small island for the sake of your souls. I am an unworthy servant of Christ but I have been called to keep watch and teach His flock. I wanted to see you and do what I can to teach you."

The old men smiled but said nothing.

"Tell me," the Bishop said, "what do you do to save your souls and how do you serve God on this island?"

The oldest hermit answered, "We do not know the best way to serve God. We only serve and support each other."

"But how do you pray to God?" asked the Bishop.

"We pray this way," replied the old hermit. "We are three just as You are the Trinity. Have mercy on us."

The other two monks repeated the prayer. "We are three and You are the Trinity. Have mercy on us."

"You have heard something about the Holy Trinity, I see," the Bishop said shaking his head. "But you do not pray correctly. Listen to me and I will teach you how to pray as the Holy Scriptures command all men to pray."

Hours passed as the Bishop quoted chapter and verse before teaching the three old hermits the precise words of the Lord's Prayer. He had them repeat each sentence after him.

"Our Father who art in Heaven hallow be thy name."

Each time a mistake was made, the Bishop started from the beginning, saying the prayer fifty times over until each of the old men could do so independently. As the moon appeared over the water and the eastern sky grew dark, the Bishop rose to return to the ship.

He embraced the hermits and kissed them, telling them to pray exactly as he had taught them. Then he got into the boat. As he returned to the ship, the Bishop could hear the hermits loudly repeating the Lord's Prayer.

The pilgrims on the ship were asleep by the time the boat reached the ship. The Bishop, however, wasn't tired. He sat alone at the stern thinking how pleased the hermits had been to learn the correct way to pray. The Bishop thanked God for bringing him to educate the three old men.

Suddenly, the Bishop was distracted from his thoughts by something white moving along the path of moonlight shinning upon the water. The Bishop stared at it, wondering if it was a seagull or a small fishing boat with a gleaming white sail.

The Bishop's eyesight was poor in the darkness and he couldn't see what it was even when it got nearer. At that moment, a sailor passed by and the Bishop beckoned to him. "Look there in the moonlight. What is it you see? I can't trust my eyes."

The sailor looked, then rubbed his eyes in disbelief. He stammered and could barely say the words.

"Oh Lord! I see the three hermits walking towards us on the water. It's as if they are walking on dry land."

All three seemed to be gliding smoothly on the water, their long white beards as bright as the moonlight.

When they reached the ship, all three raised their heads and cried out in one voice.

"We have forgotten your teaching. We were fine as long as we kept repeating it, but when we stopped to build a fire a few words dropped out. When we had our meal in silence as we usually do, a few more words fell away. Now it seems we can't remember any of it. Please, Bishop. Teach it to us again."

The Bishop made the sign of the cross. Leaning over the ship's railing, he said, "Whatever words you use will surely reach the Lord. It is you who should teach me. Please pray for all us sinners."

Then the Bishop bowed low as the three old men turned and walked back across the sea. Throughout the night, a bright light like a glimmering star could be seen on the island.

The Garden of Meditation

"In contemplation the mind

is not at pause but fully active."

— Saint Thomas Aquinas

Many roads lead to the garden gate. Each offers its own unique viewpoint along a particular path. Many different systems of meditation developed since humankind gazed up at the stars and began to wonder about the nature of the universe.

Though these different systems grew according to the time and culture where they sprouted, each form has a common goal. Everyone who takes the road to the garden gate is seeking a union with the Sacred.

A seeker finds the Garden of Meditation along one of three roads. The first is the intellectual approach when the mind beings to study the deeper meaning of what it sees. Without fully realizing it, you entered this stage just by reading this book.

Perhaps the words excite you as your mind considers new possibilities. Maybe you struggle with doubt and skepticism. Some passages may even be confusing but in the attempt to understand, the mind must consider the cryptic significance of the words. To grasp at the concepts presented on these pages, the mind translates the printed word into images and emotional impressions in order to appreciate their full meaning.

Though at this moment it takes little effort for you to read the words, remember there was a time when the ability to read came slowly. Recall the beginning, how the young mind learned to identify marks on paper as representing letters of the alphabet.

The next step was to form the letters into words, then words into complete sentences. Each stage brought about a deeper understanding as the mind learned to interpret the marks of black ink into words and ideas. Simple words led to words that were more complex. As you grew older, concepts became more intricate, ideas more complex and your ability to understand grew as your life expanded.

In spiritual contemplation, the mind looks beyond the mere physical manifestation of life. It explores that which is extrasensory. It delves into the spiritual reality underlying all of existence.

A simple form of this exploration is the second approach of daydreaming as the mind shifts its consciousness by withdrawing from its physical surroundings to embark upon an inner journey. By daydreaming, the mind creates alternative scenarios as an investigative technique. Daydreaming is the exploration of different possibilities, other ways of being in the world, and is an exercise of the mind's creative abilities.

Spiritual daydreaming is the mind contemplating a specific word or idea, sometimes a particular image or action. Contemplation is a key unlocking a hidden door that opens upon a new reality.

An example is the contemplation of icons and other forms of sacred art. Daydreaming on these images is the mind's creative and perceptive abilities seeking to connect with the Sacred. Religious imagery is never mere decoration but serves as portals through which the observer enters into the scene depicted.

Quietly considering the painted images, the contemplative monk becomes a participant. It matters little to the monk who the artist was or what type of paint was used. The monk sees more than dabs of color on a gold-leaf background, more than the style of brush strokes. Neither does the monk care for its historical or monetary value. To the monk, such things are superficial.

In the glow of candlelight illuminating the icon, the mind of the monk withdraws from physical time and space to contemplate the life of the icon and the greater meaning hidden below the surface. Like gazing into a mirror, the monk considers his own reflection, his own sense of self, his own feelings and beliefs within the context of a sacred image.

By contemplating the saints and angels, the bodhisattvas and gurus and the multitude of holy men and women, the mind of the monk searches for the spiritual reality within his or her own soul. In quiet meditation, the monk embraces the spiritual qualities represented within the icon. In solitude, the monks sits in front of the image and comes to understand that in order to truly learn from it, it is not enough to just study its form and color. The monk must embrace its mystery. By embracing it, the monk learns to experience the truth on a personal level.

The personal experience is the third approach to the Garden of Meditation. Remember the words of Jesus: *"The Kingdom of God is within."*

No longer focused on external objects, the monk looks within the depth of his or her inner being to find the Divine Light within. In the Garden of Meditation, there is much to be discovered. Wandering among the flowers, trees and garden structures, the monk learns through experience the wonders of creation and the beauty of his or her eternal soul.

In order to reach the deeper recess of the Garden, a firm foundation like stones embedded on a garden path, must be built. Otherwise, the smallest disturbance will intrude and discourage further exploration. Therefore, the following guidelines are given as stepping stones towards establishing a solid beginning.

Stepping Stones along the Path

Remember to be patient, as well as disciplined. Meditation is not a laborious task. Instead, meditation is the natural realization of your spiritual abilities adding a new dimension to everyday life.

Rather than forcing events to happen, simply allow the process to gently unfold in accordance with your personal timetable best suited for your temperament. Let go of expectations and judgments. Do not compare your experience to anything you may have read or been told. The inner journey is personal and what you experience is in accordance to the particular needs of your soul.

In the beginning, the emphasis is on the self and personal transformation. Before attempting to grasp what is universal and eternal, know yourself first. Meditation is more a matter of self-discovery than the acquisition of esoteric teachings. It is the quest for the light within your own soul.

Begin this self-exploration by trusting your feelings. Let your feelings guide you. Seek out and find a spiritual image that appeals to your feelings. Your mind can be indecisive and choosing by visual beauty alone distorts the purpose but an image that makes you feel something, an image that provokes an emotional response will stir the soul to action.

The sacred image you chose should invoke a personal response. It should resonate within you and touch your heart. As well as being a personal symbol, the spiritual image is an outward sign, a visual reminder of the new direction you've taken towards developing the greater power of spirituality in your life.

This image will be easy to find if you trust your instincts. Sometimes the image will find itself to you as when an icon will appear as a gift from a friend. Usually, however, the image will be of greater significance if it's something you consciously sought. Either way, this image is to be the initial focus for meditation.

Another helpful tool aiding the meditative state is music of a soft, non-vocal quality. Music with lyrics appeals to the side of the brain that listens and interprets the words. Instead, simple soothing melodies work best. Peaceful music calms the mind. Focusing on the tones and rhythm pulls the mind away from scattered thoughts and stimulates other areas of the brain.

The purpose of meditation is to lessen the logical, linear-thinking part of the brain and awaken the lesser used parts of the mind. Doing so increases intuition, creativity and sensory awareness beyond physical sensations.

If there is difficulty in directing a multitude of scattered thoughts towards a single purpose, the practice of repetitious prayer is often helpful. It's like a lullaby for the brain. Just know that the "thinking" brain has been developed for many years and is active throughout your waking hours. It will take time and discipline to shift into a different consciousness.

When you are ready to take the first steps towards the garden gate, establish a time during the day when you will not be disturbed. Set aside 15 minutes just for yourself. Especially beneficial is establishing the same time and place each day. A consistent time and location for meditation prepares the mind, body and spirit for the journey before you even sit down. The shift from physical reality to the spiritual then becomes a smooth transition.

Consistency in scheduling also helps deter distractions by reserving 15 minutes exclusively for you. Not only will it help you avoid making excuses for your self-imposed solitude, but also informs others that the needs of the soul are important. The demands of the world will just have to wait.

During the 15 minutes you have set aside for meditation, do nothing more than sit and relax. While some schools of meditation prescribe ritual forms of sitting, it is more important to find a comfortable position. A body forced into an awkward pose can be distracting and defeats the purpose by having you focusing on the body. There is no need for the physical body to suffer in order to reach a state of meditation. To avoid falling asleep, however, it is better in the beginning to sit upright than to lie down, if possible.

The physical body must also be taken along on the journey. Tension diverts energy away from the meditative state and therefore, relaxation is essential. A few slow, deep breaths will be helpful. Remember, meditation is not laboring towards a goal but gently allowing time for the soul to emerge.

Begin by slowly reciting your personal prayer. If you can do so without feeling self-conscious, say the words aloud. Prayer is a means of entering into a sacred frame of mind. By anointing yourself with prayer and directing your mind towards that which is holy, the soul is strengthened.

The prayer also alerts all seen and unseen forces of your intention. It is also used as psychic protection as negativity in all forms withdraws from the power and light of your spoken words. At the same time, prayer helps you align with Godly powers, with guardian angels, with saints and all other forces beneficial to your spiritual growth.

Give yourself a schedule of five consecutive days. Be disciplined even if at first you experience nothing more than boredom and restlessness. Just sit still for 15 minutes for five days. During that time, learn to focus your attention on the sacred image you adopted as your own. If other thoughts intrude, if your mind wanders, firmly and patiently redirect your focus back to the image. Gaze upon it.

Connect to the feeling it invokes. Remind yourself that meditation is a time when you listen to your own heart, to be alone with your own feelings untroubled by the demands of the world.

Practice stillness. In quiet solitude, the focus is on you. It's like gazing upon a tranquil pond and wondering what lies beneath the surface.

A Guided Meditation

Let the following words become real. Visualize the images presented. Be more than a reader but also be a participant as the words take you on a journey. The following is a guide into the Garden of Meditation.

You are walking along the bank of a river. The water flows smoothly; barely a ripple breaks the surface. There is only a soft splashing along the shore.

The sun shines brightly and the weather is perfect. The faint scent of pine trees drifts from the surrounding forest. Breathe deep as you walk. Listen to the sound of the wind in the trees. Feel sand and pebbles beneath your feet.

A short distance away, there is a small boat settled on the shore. Walk towards it. Notice its size and color. As you draw near, you'll see the bottom of the boat is lined with pillows. You will also notice there are no oars.

Get in the boat. Lie down and be comfortable. Look up at the sky, at the passing white clouds. Feel the boat gently rocking like a cradle as it pulls away from the riverbank.

The boat drifts out into the middle of the river and the water carries it along. You look up at the sky. Flowering tree branches pass overhead as the boat moves downstream. Relax. Trust the boat will take you where you need to go without any effort on your part.

Nothing else matters at this moment. The cares of the world float away as the boat carries you further along the river. Be at peace.

Eventually the boat moves towards the bank and rests upon the sand. Step out of the boat.

In front of you is a vast forest. Ancient trees tower above you. Take a moment to look. Somewhere within the forest is a path. Let your instincts guide you to find it. Just feel what direction to take.

Once you found the path, begin to walk. There is nothing to fear. This path is yours. As you walk, look around you. Notice any details: the rocks, a fallen leaf, an animal moving through the undergrowth, a tree branch swaying in the wind. Sense the warm tree bark. Breathe deeply. Smell the rich scent of earth.

Up ahead, not too far in the distance, there is a gate. On the other side of that gate is a garden. When you reach the gate, take a moment and relax. Look at the gate and notice the details: the latch, the hinges, the texture of the gate. Is it wood or metal? If it is locked, know you have the key.

When you are ready, open the gate and step into the garden.

Beyond the gate is the perfect garden, one that was created for you alone. The arrangement of flowers and trees was designed just for you.

Walk around and explore the garden. Look at the colors. Feel the sunshine. Listen for the sound of water. It might be a fountain, a waterfall, or a stream. Go find the source of the water and refresh yourself.

Be at peace.

Become familiar with your garden. Whenever you sit in meditation return to the garden. Each time you visit, you'll discover new features. As you change, so will the garden. Dormant flowers will grow. New features will be revealed. The garden grows as you grow. New flowers and trees will suddenly blossom. Hidden paths will be revealed.

Sometimes you will go to the garden to discover a mystery among the flowers. Other times, you'll go to rest and strengthen your soul. It is your garden.

Seek and You Shall Find

Going Deeper into the Garden

An oasis exists within the desert, a place of running water, of trees and flowers, a place where a weary traveler finds rest. It is the Garden of Meditation where crystal waters wash away the dust of the past and the brilliant colors of creation heal the heart. In the garden, the soul finds freedom under an endless sky of blue.

In the Garden of Meditation, the soul awakens to its own divine light. Like a phoenix rising from the ashes, the soul ascends from the chaos of scattered thoughts and conflicting emotions. Rising above temporal reality, the world of opposites, of life and death, right and wrong, up and down, the soul seeks unity with all creation.

Unfettered by the limitations of earthly existence, the soul can spread its wings and explore the spiritual power of its own true nature. In the Garden of Meditation, the liberated soul wanders, gathering a harvest of wisdom that imparts its fragrance on the mind, the body and the heart.

For the mind, it is the understanding that comes from an expanded awareness of reality. No longer dependent on the five physical senses for information, the soul develops intuition—what some people call "psychic abilities—as the "sixth sense" of the inner eye is strengthened. In meditation, the enigmatic segments of the brain, those sections of undiscovered purpose, begin to be utilized. By activating those channels of the mind through the practice of meditation, there is an experience of what is rightly called, "an altered state of being."

For the body, meditation is a time of cleansing and renewal as the energies of a higher vibration are felt internally and externally. Such energies include, but are not limited to, what is often described as an all-prevailing sense of peace.

When peace is felt internally, the physical body releases tension. The feeling of peace comforts it. Other times, the body will twitch in response to new energies. Many practitioners of meditation report a swaying or rocking motion of the body. This physical reaction during meditation can be called a "re-wiring" as the body adjusts to the new experience.

Obviously, as the body reacts to the natural forces of cold, heat and such, so it responds to unseen energies, as anyone who has ever received an electrical shock can attest. Because the body is not a separate entity but is connected with the mental and emotional aspects of the human personality, it will respond to heightened consciousness, emotional clarity and the different forms of spiritual energy. After all, love is unseen and yet, love can be felt.

For the heart, it is that love, that all-encompassing force of God from which all of creation came into being. The heart basks in that love. It is life itself. Pure love, all giving, all forgiving, all embracing, is the soul's birthright. Divine love enflaming the heart brings a greater light to all of reality.

In the Garden of Meditation, the soul plants within its own heart the seeds of hope, forgiveness, compassion and love to replace the weeds of unhealed pain, the loneliness of separation and the self-centered arrogance of the ego.

The entire self enters the garden, the physical, as well as the spiritual, the conscious and the deeper levels of awareness. The mind, body and heart participate in the quest for enlightenment. In turn, all parts benefit.

From each flower in the garden comes a fragrance to relax the body and calm the mind. From a deep well of clear water, inner strength is drawn to replenish the spirit in times of tribulation.

Love creates the garden, gives life to the trees and flowers and flowing waters. Divine Love permeates and makes holy this garden of the soul. Many seekers throughout history have come to this garden. Many paths lead to it. Though the forms of meditation differ according to cultural and personal preferences, it is still only one garden with one purpose—to develop a deeper sense of personal spirituality.

To follow the Way of the Monk is to seek the Kingdom of God within. The monk makes a conscious decision, born out of devotion and a yearning for understanding, to seek that which exits beyond the borders of time and space. Entering the spiritual oasis, a monk finds a garden of delight where nothing else seems to matter but the light of the sun, the warmth of the earth, the brilliance of color and the whisper of the wind in joyful laughter.

The Garden of Meditation is a place created for the benefit of the individual soul, a place to transcend the limited definition of the self.

Found within most monasteries is an enclosed area where a simple garden is grown. Much has been written about the peaceful atmosphere of a monastery garden where God is contemplated in the smallest herbs, the song of birds and the cycle of the seasons; all so different, all of God. Within this protected enclosure, a holy place is provided for quiet reflection. In solitude, a monk listens to the beating of his or her own heart harmonizing with the rhythms of creation. This garden also grows within the deep recesses of the monk's soul.

To wander within the Garden of Meditation takes little effort. Prayer is the key that unlocks the gate. Desire opens it. Willingness to enter the unknown, to leave behind for a time logic, ambition, personal power and control will remove any obstacle in your path.

"Come away," invited the Rabbi. "Come into the desert and rest awhile."

Meditation is leaving behind the density of the earth to a place where the soul awakens. In the garden, the soul is strengthened in ways the world cannot provide. In meditation, the soul finds refuge and strength so it can continue its journey of earthly existence.

For the soul is more than a personality shaped by social status, occupation, family heritage and physical appearance. In meditation, the soul manifests its own divine nature. In the light of God's love, the soul blossoms into the "higher self" connected to all creation. The ability to do so is within all beings. It is an innate ability, much like a seed awaiting the proper season to blossom.

Entering the inner garden is a personal, solitary endeavor, a journey into a realm unseen by the human eye, an ascent that can only be perceived by the inner being of the soul. The monk enters alone. It is not, however, a lonely endeavor. The companionship of guardian angels surrounds you. Those who have gone before will guide you. They walk with you as you discover the deeper mysteries of the garden.

Those who sincerely seek truth gain the most. The mysteries of the garden reveal themselves to the humble. Anyone entering the garden with a preconceived agenda, such as the quest for personal power, will wander off into a labyrinth of illusion and deception.

Openness to new experiences and the willingness to learn, allows the heart rather than the mind to lead. A sincere seeker with true desire to grow will avoid the pitfalls of ego gratification.

That is not to say you will not stumble. Sometimes you will fall. There are risks involved. Many enthusiastic promoters of meditation fail to mention its potential danger. In the past, someone with the experience of having walked the path would guide the novice monk into its deeper mysteries.

In the Jewish mystical tradition of the Kabbala, only those judged to be mature and mentally stable were allowed passage into its mysteries. Buddhist monks are required to build a firm foundation of knowledge to guide them along the path of inner awareness. Within Western Christianity, mystical revelation is put through a rigorous examination before being accepted. It is well known that what the mind can perceive, the mind can also distort.

Therefore, the Way of the Monk is to enter the garden carrying the staff of sincerity and perseverance to push aside the undergrowth and remove any rocks barring the way. Meditation is a quest. The monk knows that sometimes he or she will have to face any inner fears that block progress. Coming upon the obstacles of fear, the monk has but one option—to confront and overcome it. To turn back is to surrender to fear.

Confronting the fear encourages the development of the soul's inner strength. Within all souls is a resilience, a flexibility and a steadfastness to share in all that creation has to offer. The soul knows its existence is directly dependent on the Source of All Creation, that which we call God. The soul takes that reassurance wherever it roams.

Without inner strength found in the soul's connection to God, the garden path can be rocky. There are many who have abandoned the practice of meditation due to fear, confusion and disappointment. They have little understanding that the spiritual realm is a complex journey that unfolds slowly. With patience and persistence, the monk continues to explore the intricate byways of the garden, knowing each new crossroads on the path will offer new revelations.

In meditation, the monk peels away the restrictions of physical reality and enters a garden realm where seasons can change in a moment, where roses grow from seeds in a sudden burst of creativity, where rivers run swift or slow and each day a new sense of self can be discovered.

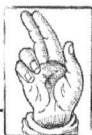

Saint Seraphim

They sat together in silence slowly sipping an aromatic tea served in cracked mugs. The nobleman and the monk faced each other. The hut was small and smelled of dry thatch, worn wood and warm candle wax. A large brown bear sat in the doorway licking its paws as it watched the monk with a look that could only be described as affection. The bear made the nobleman nervous but not as tense as the monk made him feel.

Thousands of people seeking the monk's advice had made their way deep into the forest wilderness. Many stories were told about the holy man of the forest. It was said that twice the Mother of Christ cured him of illness, that he would spend entire days and nights perched on a boulder with his arms raised to Heaven and that all sorts of wild animals came to him as docile as an old hunting dog. The nobleman had seen this for himself when the brown bear ambled into the hut and ate from the monk's own hand.

For many years, he was just an ordinary monk. He entered the Sarov monastery at the age of 18 wearing a large copper crucifix his mother had given him. When he took his monastic vows at the age of 27, he was given the name Seraphim, which in Hebrew means "Burning" or "Fiery."

As he immersed himself in the life of a monk, he began to have visions of angels. During a Holy Thursday liturgy, he saw Christ enter the church to bless all who were there. Overwhelmed by the sight, Saint Seraphim could not speak for three days.

Later in life, with the blessings of his spiritual teacher, Saint Seraphim withdrew into the forest. In self-imposed seclusion, he began his battle with darkness both human and demonic. Once he was beaten so badly by bandits that for the rest of his life he walked with a staff for support.

After many years in isolation, Mother Mary appeared to the monk and asked him to open his door and his heart to the many people who would soon arrive seeking spiritual advice.

The nobleman was just one of the numerous pilgrims who came to the hut in the forest. What he experienced became one of the most profound writings of the modern Orthodox Church. His name was Nicholas Alexandrovich Motovilov.

"How can I see the grace of the Holy Spirit?" Motovilov asked. "How can I know if the Holy Spirit is with me or not?"

Saint Seraphim tried to explain using the lives of the saints and apostles as examples. He talked about grace and divine light. He spoke of holy peace and perfect love.

"Christ calls it a peace which comes from His own generosity and is not of this world," said the old monk. "No temporary earthly success can give it to the human heart. It is what the Lord gave to His disciples saying, 'My peace I give to you.' It is called the Peace of God."

The nobleman didn't understand. "I want that peace but how can someone have the experience?"

"To obtain internal peace requires silence," Saint Seraphim said. "And, as much as possible, keep a constant conversation with oneself and speak to others sparingly."

The nobleman looked into the monk's eyes as if to find understanding within the fire of his glance. He struggled to grasp the old monk's teaching. Saint Seraphim, who was said to have the gift of clairvoyance, could see both the desire for a spiritual life and the obstacles that held the nobleman trapped by his social status.

Reaching out, Saint Seraphim took Motovilov by the shoulders and said, "Spiritual life is the awareness of a person within himself and the contemplation of the hidden working of his own heart."

"But how does a person know?"

The old monk shook the nobleman and laughed. "We are both now, my dear fellow, in the Holy Spirit."

Later in life, the nobleman recalled what happened. "After those words were spoken, I glanced at his face and there came over me an even greater reverent awe. Imagine the center of the sun, the dazzling light of its midday rays. It was the same brilliance on the monk's face.

"I could see the movement of his lips and the changing expression of his eyes. I could hear his voice. I felt his hands on my shoulders but I could not see his hands. I couldn't even see myself or the monk holding me; only a blinding light spreading far around, illuminating the hut, spreading outside to the snow covering the forest glade. Even the falling snowflakes seemed on fire. You can imagine the state I was in!

"I felt such calmness and peace in my soul. No words can express it."

Saint Seraphim died eight years after opening his door to pilgrims. He died kneeling in front of an icon of the Blessed Mother.

Devotion

"Accustom yourself to continually

make many acts of love,

for they enflame and melt the soul."

— Saint Theresa of Avila

Devotion is not a labor of the mind forcing itself to follow rules under the burden of feeling obligated. True devotion comes freely from a passionate heart.

Christian and Buddhist monks chant their devotion.

Sufi Dervishes dance.

Orthodox Hindus recite mantras at dawn and again at dusk.

In the homes of Greek and Russian Orthodox Christians, an oil lamp glows in front of treasured icons of Christ and the family's patron saint.

Devotion is like a rose garden. As there are countless varieties of roses, acts of Devotion also take many forms and for numerous reasons. In joy and sorrow, in gratitude and struggle, all acts of Devotion have the common root of love.

Because acts of Devotion are acts of love, they are not hidden away as if something embarrassing, nor are they used as a display of one's piety. Devotion is a part of daily life, a relationship between you and the Divine. Devotion is expressed with the same intimacy shared with a beloved. It is an outward form of communication.

Nothing in the universe requires Devotion. It is not a demand. Devotion is for the soul, a compass along the road of life on earth, a staff to assist you on your long journey.

Devotion will be needed at times to face the challenges and obstacles along the spiritual path, some even more difficult than if you'd chosen an easier road. Strength and determination are elements of Devotion to help you stay true to what Jesus called "the narrow road."

In his words, *"The Kingdom of God can be entered only through the narrow gate. The road to destruction is broad and its gate is wide enough for many. But the gateway to life and road beyond is narrow and only a few ever find it."*

It will not be easy. But, then again, what way of life is without trouble?

What is not difficult, however, is knowing how to be devoted. People are devoted to their jobs, their family, even their pets. They are faithful to a sports team, fanatical about a television program and can become obsessive about what they eat. All are forms of devotion to a particular way of being.

Devotion to spiritual growth is no different. It is a commitment to a way that is unique and often contrary to the ways of the world. And that is the first and perhaps biggest challenge: to go against what is considered normal and acceptable in order to follow an unknown path.

It is difficult but worthwhile. People dedicate themselves to lesser goals. What makes such pursuits lesser is the temporal nature of the object of their devotion. Television programs end. Sport teams win and lose. Even cuisine follows fads. Things of this world may change but they never expand beyond their basic nature.

The soul, however, does not change so much as develops its capabilities, becomes stronger and increases its light. Devotion is dedicating your life on earth towards that goal. The resulting benefits cannot wane, cannot be taken away or fade with time. The profits of Devotion are eternal.

To reap the greater rewards, true Devotion integrates the mind, the emotions and the physical body towards a single purpose. Each aspect of the human experience must be involved to bring the entire physical being in alignment with the soul.

Every part of you must be in agreement. Sacrifices will be made on all levels and if one part of you is not committed to the task, the road will be more difficult. Obstacles will seem insurmountable. Opposition will seem undefeatable. Sacrificing whatever holds you back, whatever limits you, will be more painful than necessary without the commitment of Devotion.

True Devotion will demand sacrifices.

Consider the words of Meister Eckhart. *"God is not found in the soul by adding anything but rather by the method of subtraction."*

Sacrifices are made every day by all people. Time and energy are sacrificed for the sake of a job. How often do people go to work even when sick or when they'd just rather do something else? Parents sacrifice themselves for their children, giving up their own pleasures so to nurture and provide for their child. How many will sacrifice money in the hope of winning the lottery? And yet, how few are willing to make sacrifices for their own spiritual growth.

Therefore, the first step is making a mental commitment. At this moment, you stand at a crossroads, one of many. You can close this book right now and forget about it or you can finish what you started. You have no idea what is on the next page and yet, you're willing to find out.

And so it is with spirituality. You will not always know what lies ahead but with a Devotion to the path taken, you'll place one foot in front of the other and continue to explore and discover.

No one really knows what the future holds. You may have expectations. You think you know what is supposed to happen. You know what society and religion has promised, as if life was a formula. Do this or that and you'll be rewarded with prosperity, happiness and security.

How many have come to learn otherwise? How many marriages were not "made in Heaven?" How many secure careers ended abruptly? How much disappointment comes from chasing after the promises of the world? So much time and energy devoted to pursuing an ideal that is always just out of reach. Even if successful, it eventually comes to an end.

The Way of the Monk offers no promises, no guarantee of salvation and no fast track to enlightenment. Devotion to spiritual growth leads to only that——self-development of the soul. It is a path of discovery about your true nature and it's connection to the Source of All Life.

The mental decision to follow the path is to have the willingness to take the narrow path, to walk into the unknown, to be willing to explore.

If the thought of going beyond the veil to seek the mysterious, if the idea of finding what is invisible to the human eye causes you to feel fearful, then good. Feel the fear but don't give it power.

The second level of Devotion is making the emotional commitment to stay on the path in spite of any fears and doubts. As you go beyond all you've been taught about reality, as you break past the limitations of who you think you are and defy definitions, there will times of confusion and fear. It is to be expected.

However, these feeling should not deter you. An emotional vow of steadfastness keeps you moving forward. Should you falter and fall, emotional Devotion helps you to stand again.

Whether you lose focus and trip over a distraction or something comes along to knock you down, you will rise again. Devotion insists that you get back on your feet.

Though you feel fear, you keep on walking. When there is doubt, do not waver. The emotional promise you've made will give you strength to overcome all obstacles and opposition. You'll continue what you started because deep inside you know there is no choice. It must be done. You get up and continue on your way because of the promise you made to yourself.

Even a small gesture of Devotion will help you find the strength. Lighting a candle, placing a flower in front of a favored image, making the sign of the cross or attending a religious service are all physical expressions of Devotion.

The division between spiritual and physical is an illusion. The human body is also a manifestation of Sacred Creativity. The voice, the hands, even the feet can convey holiness on earth. A voice sings, prays and speaks in the language of sacred energy when it speaks in Tongues, as it is called. Hands bless, heal and reach up to the heavens. Feet dance, jump and twirl to express the joy of the soul.

The body is an instrument capable of more than can be imagined. It is a part of everything that surrounds you, no different from the distant mountains or a single rose held in your hand. The body is a river and ocean, stars and planets. It is a small but beautiful part of creation, playing its part in the vast intricacy of Life. To consider the body separate from God is to cause division within the self and a barrier against total integration.

For that reason, the third vow of Devotion is consecrating the body to express spirituality with discernible action. Grasping your hands as you pray aloud is an example. Clapping your hands and dancing to a gospel song is another. All religious rites and rituals serve the purpose of allowing the physical body to show Devotion.

It is true that over time traditional rituals can lose the power of the sacred moment. Repetition quenches the fire. Familiarity dulls it. Forced obligation to a set of rites becomes a burden rather than an expression of Devotion.

The movements, the gestures and the words become a pantomime of what once held great power.

Without Devotion of mind and emotions, physical acts become insipid. It is not enough to watch another perform a ritual or to participate by following prescribed motions. Your total being, the focus of your mind and the feeling in your heart gives real power to the act. Your Devotion can sanctify the air around you, bless the atmosphere and change energy to a higher vibration.

The act itself doesn't have to be complicated. Nor does it have to involve the use of elaborate objects. Lighting a plain white candle can become a powerful demonstration of Devotion when done with great love.

Creating a Ritual

People perform rituals without realizing their actions are a series of daily rites. Bathing rituals, food preparation ceremonies, the repetition of work routines, even leisure celebrations follow customary formats.

The Way of the Monk includes acts of Devotion as a physical connection to the sacred facet of life. It can be as simple as touching an icon before leaving your home or spending time in a church or temple.

Many of the old folk traditions of Devotion have disappeared. People visited roadside shrines to light candles, place flowers and pray. Statues of favored saints were common in many homes. Church bells rang throughout the day, not just to announce the hour but as a reminder to take a moment to pray.

Some people may think those actions as quaint at best and useless at worse. Such rituals, however, served to bring holiness into the lives of those surrounded by the hectic and clamorous intrusions of the world.

In that moment when fingertips touch the plaster robe of a saint, when a candle flame flicker in the dark or

when a bouquet of flowers is placed in a vase and offered as a gift of love, those simple acts of Devotion merged the transitory with the eternal.

The act itself isn't important. The power of the act is your personal involvement. It may seem awkward at first so find an act of Devotion that is simple, easy to remember and means something to you personally. Make it a daily practice.

A simple act is like a seed. In time, it will grow. At the right time, it will bear fruit. Nourished by that fruit, you'll be able to perform the greatest act of Devotion.

When mind, emotion and body are in accord, every moment in your life becomes an act of Devotion.

As Christ taught, *"Let your light shine before men so they may see your good works which glorify your Father in heaven."*

You become the light that dispels darkness.

Be warned. The light within you is a fire. Some people will be drawn to its brilliance and warmth. Others will fear it. Most people will not even see the fire. Nevertheless, the light continues to shine because it is fueled by Devotion and not the reactions of others.

That is true Devotion, making your entire life an act of sincere consecration to a force greater than the self, more intricate than anything on earth and more powerful than anything created by man.

Devotion is renewal. It is a marriage vow said every day. It is baptism and confirmation. Devotion is your soul in communion with God.

The Artist

Fra Angelico ("Angelic Friar) as he is commonly known today was born Guido di Pietro around 1395 near Fiesole in the Tuscan area of Italy. Even before joining the Dominican order, he was acknowledged as a talented artist.

During his life, Fra Angelico illuminated manuscripts, painted frescoes in the chapels of the Vatican, decorated monasteries with the lives of the saints and painted altarpieces, helping to shift artistic expression from the Gothic style towards the period known as the Early Renaissance.

The biographer of artists Vasari wrote this: "In their bearing and expression, the saints painted by Fra Angelico come nearer to the truth than the figures done by any other artist."

Vasari also added, "It is impossible to bestow too much praise on this holy father, who was so humble and modest in all he did and said and whose pictures were painted with such talent and piety."

Fra Angelico is purported to say he "painted not for time or for men but for eternity and God."

In 1982, Pope John Paul II beatified Fra Angelico and two years later declared him to be the patron of Catholic artists.

Fra Angelico's epitaph asks that he not be praised for his talents, but "say rather in the name of Christ, I gave all I had to the poor. Thus part of my work remains on earth and part in Heaven."

The bells would ring soon, the call to evening prayer. He'd put down his brush and join his brothers, usually happy to do so but if only he could finish painting what he saw so clearly, a vision so real, so heartbreaking.

The artist wiped the tears from his eyes with the sleeve of his robe.

The brush he held, the brush tipped with vivid red pigment, was poised in midair. He always hesitated before adding the detail of blood.

When he touched the brush to His feet, the artist felt a stabbing pain in his own feet. Painting the blood pouring from the wound in His side made him moan and when the brush touched the palm in each hand, the artist willed himself to hold the brush steady, though it hurt him to do so.

And all the while he wept. Every time the artist painted Him on the cross, tears streaked his cheeks. He had painted countless scenes of the crucifixion and it was always the same pain and tears.

With each commission of a fresco or altarpiece, the vision became clearer and the pain sharper. It was as if he was standing at the foot of the cross. On wood panels or monastery walls, he tried to bring the reality of his vision into the present, to help other see the taunt muscles of His arms stretched upon the cross, the painful piercing of nails and the anguish of those who had to watch the agony of their Beloved.

The artist bore the pain of his painting, accepting the ache in his heart. It was a small sacrifice compared to the one he painted.

When one of his assistants, a young friar with considerable talent, asked him why he cried whenever he painted a crucifix, the artist replied, "When you paint the life of Christ, you must be with Christ."

It was the same with his other paintings. He experienced whatever he painted. A fresco of the Annunciation filled him with the same awe, fear and eventual acceptance as Mary felt at the sight and speech of the Angel Gabriel. The Nativity transported him to a place of fresh hay and straw, the musky aroma of ox and donkey, the bleating of sheep and the quiet curiosity of shepherds.

A panel depicting Madonna and child was done with a caressing brushstroke, gentle dabs of paints applied with a maternal love.

And, when he portrayed the lives of the saints, he walked among them, wandering the desert, strolling along the cloister, suffering through their trials, sharing their ecstasy as they gazed upon the glory of God.

Before he began the rudimentary sketches of a subject, a portal opened that diminished time and space so that the object of his devotion was there with him. The door opened with prayer.

Afterwards, when the brushes were cleaned, the paint pots sealed and the candles snuffed, the artist said another prayer, one of thanksgiving for having been given the grace to experience the connection to those who lived so long ago. He gave thanks for the rewards of his devotion, to experience the holiness that exists between creator and creation, to feel the sacredness of tears and joy and be blessed with the task of bringing the Holy Ones into the lives of the observers.

Vesper bells rang in the distant and the artist put away the tools of his devotion. He took a quick look at the altarpiece while removing his paint-dappled smock.

"It is finished," he murmured.

The last words of Christ: It is finished.

The body, pale and tinged gray, was being taken from the cross. The face looked at rest, asleep after a long day's labor, no longer in the world, no longer suffering from the torture of the scourging, the sharp nails, the final thrust of the spear.

Men gently lower the body as if careful to avoid adding more harm to Him who endured so much pain. Women stand ready with the shroud. One woman kisses the blood-streaked feet. Angels emerge from clouds and look on.

The Deposition, the descent from the cross, was the artist's most complex work so far. Distant hills fade into an unseen continuity that spanned oceans and continents. A city on the left side of the background echoed ancient Jerusalem and Medieval Florence, merging past with the contemporary.

In the foreground, a youth knelt with one hand held out as if to grasp the moment, the other hand touching his heart as if to keep it from bursting forth.

In that lone figure shown in profile, the artist had allegorized the devotion of his own soul.

Distant Voices Still Echo

The following quotes are the words of those who knew and helped create the Way of the Monk. Their voices echo throughout time to inspire, encourage and uplift.

Come to these pages and listen to their voices whenever you feel the need. Let their words echo within your heart.

THE CALL

"Clamoring up the mountain path, the trail goes on and on. The long gorge is choked with weeds and rocks, the creek is wide, the grass shrouded in mist. Though there hasn't been rain, the moss is slippery. The pine trees sing though but there is no wind. Who will leap the world's constraints and sit with me among the white clouds?"

— Han Shan

"The attainment of holiness is not the exclusive business of monks, as certain people think. People with families are also called to holiness, as are those in all kinds of professions, who live in the world, since the commandment about perfection and holiness is given not only to monks, but to all people."

— Hieromartyr Onuphry Gagaluk

"The calling of man by God to his supernatural end is not simply a call from without. The Divine Call has already sounded in depths of human nature."

— R. P. Brisbois

"The City of God has its foundations in every place of human habitation. Always remember, the Kingdom of God is within."

— Saint Antony Abbot

"How could the soul not take flight when, from the glorious presence, a soft call flows sweet as honey and whispers, 'Rise up now and come away.'"

— Rumi

"The spiritual path wrecks the body and afterwards restores it to health. It destroys the house to unearth the treasure, and with that treasure, builds it better than before."

— Rumi

"Let us remember that within us there is a palace of immense magnificence."

— Saint Teresa of Avila

"One of the marvels of the world is the sight of a soul sitting in prison with the key in its hand."

— Rumi

THE WAY

"We do not walk to God with the feet of our body, nor would wings, if we had them, carry us to Him, but we go to Him by the affections of our soul."

— Saint Augustine

"Spirituality is not learned by fleeing from the world, by running away from things or by remaining solitary and removed from the world. Instead, you must develop an inner solitude wherever you are, no matter who is with you. You must learn to look deeper and find God everywhere."

— Meister Eckhart

"To reach something good it is very useful to have gone astray, and thus acquire experience."

— St Teresa of Avila

"Lord, lock me up in the deepest depths of your heart; Hold me there, burn me, purify me, set me on fire, sublimate me till I become utterly what you would have me be. . ."

— Pierre Teilhard De Chardin

"If you are what you should be you will set the whole world ablaze."

- St. Catherine of Siena

"Go forth, and set the world on fire."

- St. Ignatius of Loyola

"We have within us deeply rooted weaknesses, passions, and defects. This cannot all be cut out with one sharp motion, but patience, persistence, care and attention. The path leading to perfection is long. Pray to God so that he will strengthen you. Patiently accept your falls and, having stood up, immediately run to God, not remaining in that place where you have fallen. Do not despair if you keep falling into your old sins. Many of them are strong because they have received the force of habit. Only with the passage of time and with fervor will they be conquered. Don't let anything deprive you of hope."

— St. Nectarios of Aegina

"Solitude, prayer, love and abstinence are the four wheels of the vehicle that carries our sprit heavenward."

— Saint Seraphim of Sarov

HUMILITY

"If you are humble, nothing will touch you, neither praise nor disgrace, because you know who you are."

— Mother Teresa

"Humility is to the virtues what the chain is to the rosary. Remove the chain and all the beads escape. Take away humility and all virtues disappear."

— The Cure d'Ars

"Just as it is impossible to be at the same moment both a plant and a seed, so it is impossible for us to be surrounded by worldly honor and at the same time bear heavenly fruit."

—Amma Syncletica

"I have seen all the snares of the enemy spread out over the world and I said with a groan, 'Who can get through such snares?'

Then I heard a voice say to me, 'Humility.'"

— St Antony Abbot

Acts of Devotion

"The devout man does not only believe, but feels, there is a Deity. He has actual sensations of him; his experience concurs with his reason; he sees him more and more in all his intercourses with him, and even in this life almost loses his faith in conviction."

— Joseph Addison

"The saints are like various trees, each bearing different fruit, but watered from the same source. The practices of one saint differ from those of another, but the same Spirit works in them."

— An unknown desert monk

"Genuine devotion is consistent with every state in life. Like liquid poured into a container, it adapts itself to any shape."

— J. P. Camus

Meditation

"Contemplation is nothing else but a secret, peaceful and loving infusion of God, which, if admitted, will set the soul on fire with the spirit of love."

— Saint John of the Cross

"Recall yourself sometimes to the interior solitude of your heart, and there, removed from all creatures, treat of the affairs of your salvation and your perfection with God, as a friend would speak heart to heart with another."

— St. Francis of Sales

"Come now, turn aside for a while from your daily cares, and escape for a moment from the tumult of your thoughts. Put aside your weighty concerns. Let your burdensome distractions wait. Free yourself awhile for God and rest in Him.

Enter the inner chamber of your soul. Shut out everything except God and that which can help you in seeking Him. When the door is shut, seek Him. Now, with your whole heart, say to God, 'I seek your love, Lord. It is your love I seek.'"

— Saint Anslem

"Let a man return to himself, and there in the center of his soul, let him wait upon God as one who listens to another speaking as if from a high tower, as though he had God in his heart, as though in the whole of creation there was only God and his soul."

— Saint Peter of Alcantara

"As it is impossible to verbally describe the sweetness of honey to one who has never tasted honey, so the goodness of God cannot be clearly communicated by way of teaching. We ourselves must enter into the goodness of the Lord by our own experience."

— St. Basil the Great

"Place your mind before the mirror of eternity! Place your soul in the brilliance of glory! And transform your entire being into the image of the Godhead Itself through contemplation."

— St. Clare of Assisi

"The soul is made of love and must ever strive to return to love. Therefore, it can never find rest or happiness in other things. It must lose itself in love. By its very nature it must seek God, who is love."

— Mechtild of Magdeburg

"By interior recollection we retire into God, or draw God within ourselves. But when and where can we have recourse to it? At all times, and in all places. Neither repast, nor company, nor change, nor occupation can hinder it, as neither does it hinder or interfere with any action. On the contrary, it is a salt which seasons every kind of meat, or a sugar which spoils no sauce. It consists only in interior looks between the soul and God."

— St. Francis of Sales

"I need to be silent for a while; worlds are forming in my heart."

— Meister Eckhart

"Every Christian needs a half hour of prayer each day, except if you are busy. Then you need an hour."

— Saint Francis de Sales

PRAYER

"Prayer makes

a sour heart sweet,

a sad heart merry,

a poor heart rich,

a dull heart wise,

a timid heart bold,

a weak heart strong,

a blind heart seeing,

a cold heart burning.

It draws the great God down into the small heart. It drives a hungry soul to the full God. It brings together the two lovers, God and soul, into a blissful place where they speak much of love."

— Mechtild of Magdeburg

"Everyone who asks something of God and does not receive it doubtless does not receive it for one of these reasons: either because they ask before the time, or they ask unworthily, or out of vainglory, or because if they received what they asked they would become proud or fall into negligence."

— St. John of the Ladder

Do not forsake prayer, for just as the body becomes weak when it is deprived of food, so also the soul when it is deprived of prayer draws nigh to weakness and noetic death.

— St. Gennadius of Constantinople

"When we pray to God we must be seeking nothing — nothing."

— Saint Francis of Assisi

In the World, Not of the World

"A joyful heart is more easily made perfect than one that is cast down."

— St. Philip Neri

"You were guiding me as a helmsman steers a ship, but the course you steered was beyond my understanding."

— Saint Augustine

"If you seek to be comforted, forget those who are better off than you and think of those worse off."

— Meister Eckhart

"If you find that there is no love in you, but you want to have it, then do deeds of love, even though you do them without love in the beginning. The Lord will see your desire and striving and will put love in your heart."

— St. Ambrose of Optina

"Forget your good deeds as soon as possible ... Do not record your good deeds, for if you record them, they will soon fade. But if you forget them, they will be written in eternity."

— St. Nicholas of Serbia

"Those who consciously love God in their hearts never lose an intense longing for spiritual illumination, until they feel it in their bones and no longer know themselves, but are completely transformed by the love of God.

They are both present in this life and not present.

They live in the body but have departed from it. In love, they ceaselessly journey in their souls towards God.

Their hearts constantly burn with the fire of love and they cling to God with an irresistible fervor, for they have, once and for all, transcended self-love in their love for God."

— Saint Diadochos of Photiki

"Let nothing disturb you. Let nothing dismay you. All things pass. God never changes. Patience attains all it strives for. He who has God finds he lacks nothing. God alone suffices."

— St Teresa of Avila

The greatest medicine is the emptiness of everything.

The greatest action is not conforming to the world's ways.

The greatest magic is transmuting the passions.

The greatest generosity is non-attachment.

The greatest goodness is a peaceful mind.

The greatest patience is humility.

The greatest effort is not concerned with results.

The greatest meditation is a mind that lets go.

The greatest wisdom is seeing through appearances.

— Atisha

"Let your love flow outward through the universe,

to its height, its depth, its broad extent,

a limitless love, without hatred or enmity.

Then as you stand or walk,

sit or lie down,

as long as you are awake,

strive for this with a one-pointed mind;

your life will bring heaven to earth."

— Sutta Nipata

"The saints in each generation, joined with those who have gone before, and filled like them with light, become a golden chain, in which each saint is a separate link, united to the next by faith, works and love."

— Simeon the Theologian

"He may wear costly clothing, or none.

He may be dressed in deer or tiger skin

or clothed in pure knowledge.

He may seem like a madman, or like a child,

or sometimes an unclean spirit.

Thus he wanders the earth.

Sometimes he appears to be a fool,

sometimes a wise man.

Sometimes he seems splendid as a king,

sometimes feeble-minded.

Sometimes he is calm and silent.

Sometimes he draws men to him

as a python draws its prey.

Sometimes people honor him greatly,

sometimes they insult him,

sometimes they ignore him.

That is how the illumined soul lives,

always absorbed in the highest bliss."

— Shankara

ABOUT THE AUTHOR

"It's the message not the messenger that is important," Vincent Cole often says. Nevertheless, to satisfy people's curiosity, he offers this statement.

"When people ask me how I came upon the spiritual path, I reply, 'Screaming and kicking all the way.' Before certain experiences led me down a different road, I was everything society rejected and religion judged as wrong. I have no regrets about my 'previous' life. In fact, I admit it was a lot of fun. Most of all it gave to me a greater understanding of life on this planet and a deeper compassion for the struggles of humanity.

But I discovered something better, more meaningful and worthwhile than what the world had to offer. It hasn't been easy and each day I feel as if I am just beginning.

"What I write is simply sharing things I have experienced and to express the simple message that there is more to life than what we've been led to believe. No matter who you are or what you've done in the past or where you come from, there is a path leading to great exploration and wondrous discovery. You just have to take the next step and enter the garden."

Other Titles by Vincent Cole

The Next Step in Evolution – a personal guide.

What God Said to the Rose – a guide to natural spirituality.

Desert Monk Press
Tucson, Arizona
monksbook.com